Preaching and Reading the Old Testament Lessons:

With an Eye to the New

Cycle C

Elizabeth Achtemeier

CSS Publishing Company, Inc., Lima, Ohio

Library of Congress Cataloging-in-Publication Data

Achtemeier, Elizabeth Rice, 1926-
    Preaching and reading the Old Testament lessons : with an eye to the new, Cycle B /
Elizabeth Achtemeier.
    p. cm.
    ISBN 0-7880-1870-1 (alk. paper)
    1. Bible. O.T.—Homiletical use. I. Title.
BS1191.5 .A235   2001
251'.6—dc21   2001037905
                                                                          CIP

For more information about CSS Publishing Company resources, visit our website at
www.csspub.com.

ISBN 0-7880-1943-0

*"The word of God
will stand
forever."*

Table Of Contents

Introduction

This volume contains 77 homiletical expositions of the Old Testament lessons (including the stated Lutheran options during the Pentecost season) in Cycle C of the Revised Common Lectionary. All of these were originally published by CSS Publishing Company in their magazine intended for pastors, *Emphasis*, beginning in the November/December 1997 issue (Volume 28, Number 4) and extending through the November/December 1998 issue (Volume 29, Number 4). Because the stated lectionary lessons change little from year to year, it was decided to assemble these expositions into one volume for the use of pastors, homiletical instructors, and interested lay people. The volume for Cycle B was published in 2002. The volume dealing with Cycle A will come out in 2004.

The expositions contained here are not intended as substitutes for the minister's own sermon preparation, nor are they complete sermons, although they are written in a homiletical style. Rather, they are intended for the church and are brief presentations of the kergymatic meaning of the stated texts in their historical contexts and in relation to the New Testament. They are intended to stimulate the development of truly biblical sermons, anchored in the biblical texts and related to our common life. But their messages also should be useful for private or group study of the stated texts and for homiletical instruction in the methods of explicating the Bible's message.

Much attention is given not only to the historical but also to the canonical contexts of the various texts. I am very aware of the fact that the Old Testament is an unfinished book, with many of its motifs and theologies left incomplete and its divine promises left unfulfilled. Very often, therefore, the exposition moves into the New Testament and a discussion of the work of our Lord. In addition, there are frequent citations in parentheses of other Old and New Testament texts related to the passage under discussion. If the reader will consult such citations, the Bible's own interpretation of itself will be illumined, the reader's knowledge will be enlarged, and preachers will be furnished with a wealth of sermonic material related to the text for the day.

Unless noted, the biblical text used is the RSV (Revised Standard Version), with very limited reference to other translations. The New Revised Standard Version (NRSV) has not been used because it is my view, and the view of many other scholars, that while there are no objections to the generic language used in the NRSV, that version sometimes softens the meaning or alters the structures of the biblical texts found in the original Hebrew and Greek of the scriptures. Similarly, I do not employ the New International Version (NIV), which seems to be the favorite of conservatives in the church. After working very closely with the NIV and comparing it to the original Hebrew of the Old Testament, I found that it sometimes omits important words in its translation from the Hebrew or occasionally resorts almost to a paraphrase of the original text. (See my commentary, *Minor Prophets I*, *New International Biblical Commentary*, Hendrickson Publishers, 1996.)

As I have studied these biblical texts and written these expositions I have continually been enlightened and fed by the Word of God. Sometimes that word has taken me in directions I never intended when I first sat down to write. The Word of God has more power than any interpreter of it can ever convey, and no expositions such as these can adequately mediate that saving power. There is no substitute for reading and studying and meditating and praying the biblical texts for ourselves. And there is no substitute for letting the texts themselves shape the sermon, the teaching, and the proclamation of the gospel. If this volume simply stimulates the study and aids in the announcement of the biblical word for our time, it will have been worth the effort involved in its writing.

— Elizabeth Achtemeier
Richmond, Virginia

First Sunday in Advent

Jeremiah 33:14-16

Promises are so important! We know, for example, that when we make a child a promise, we must keep it at all costs, or the child will lose all trust in us and our word. We also know that if we do not keep a promise to a friend, we may lose that friendship.

Certainly we make promises through all our life. One of the most important ones is made when we stand before a minister to be married. There we promise to love and comfort, to honor and keep our spouse, in sickness and in health. And we promise that we will forsake all others and be faithful to that marital partner as long as we both shall live.

We even have the organization of "Promise Keepers" these days — thousands of men who meet together in conferences, and who promise to be good and faithful husbands, and to instill in their home life piety and trustworthiness and love.

Sometimes we keep our promises, but sometimes we do not. Sometimes our words are just empty pledges, having no influence on our life and actions. And often times, we live in regret and guilt that we have not kept some spoken word. We think a person who keeps his or her word is a person to be honored and trusted, and we deplore and rue the times when we fail to be thus trustworthy.

We even might say that there is only One who perfectly keeps his promises, and if we study the scriptures, we find that One is God. Throughout the Bible, God is a promise-keeping God. "The Word of our God will stand forever," Second Isaiah proclaims (Isaiah 40:8). My word "shall not return to me empty, but it shall accomplish that which I purpose," God vows (Isaiah 55:11). And the whole record of the scriptures tells us that is true.

So it is too with the promise to which the Lord refers here in Jeremiah 33:14-15. Over 400 years before the time of Jeremiah, God promised King David that he would establish the davidic reign

11

forever (2 Samuel 7:13). "Your house and your kingdom shall be made sure for ever before me," God vowed. "Your throne shall be established forever" (v. 16). And then a hundred years before the time of Jeremiah, God renewed that promise: "There shall come forth a shoot from the stump of Jesse, and a branch shall grow out of his roots" (Isaiah 11:1). In like fashion here in our Jeremiah text, God makes the promise once again: "In those days and at that time I will cause a righteous Branch to spring forth for David" (Jeremiah 33:15). A davidic king to sit upon the throne! God guaranteed it by his word!

What God guarantees Israel and Judah in this text, however, is not just a davidic king. It is a *righteous* descendant of David. For it was very important that the king whom God raised up should be a righteous ruler.

There is no doubt that rulers, presidents, and leaders of nations and societies often determine the quality of life for those over whom they rule. A despot in Africa, who is interested only in gaining wealth for himself, can ruin the economy of his nation and plunge his people into poverty. An immoral president in a democracy can undermine the morality of a society and make it think that any style of life is acceptable, because even its president is abandoning ethical rules. A thieving and lying political or religious leader can lead his or her followers into equal deception that mimics the leader's perfidy.

The same was true in the life of biblical Israel. Repeatedly we find in the history of Israel's kings the phrase that says some king "made Israel to sin" (e.g. 1 Kings 15:34; 1 Kings 16:26, *et al*). Thus, when the king was unrighteous, Israel too was unrighteous in the eyes of God. Israel's life was bound up with the life of its king. The king was Israel. Israel was the king. And that people's whole fate from the hands of God depended on whether or not a righteous king ruled on the throne.

Israel did have a couple of decent and good kings, such as Josiah and Hezekiah, both of whom carried out sweeping religious reforms. But most of Israel's kings were not righteous, and that was especially true in the time of Jeremiah. Jehoiakim was a despot, introducing all sorts of syncretistic worship into Judah, oppressing the poor, and persecuting the prophets. Judah's final king before the Babylonian exile, Zedekiah, was nothing more than a puppet of the Babylonian empire. Thus, through the ages before that and even after, when it seemed that the throne would never be occupied again, Israel looked for a righteous and just ruler. Of every king who ascended the davidic throne or who claimed it, the question was asked, "Are you the one who is to come, or should we look for another?" Are you the long-awaited Branch of the davidic house, whom God promised us so long ago?

God is a promise-keeper, whose word is good forever. Therefore on this first Sunday of Advent, we eagerly await the day when we may celebrate the birth of Jesus Christ, who is the fulfillment of this age-old promise of a davidic ruler. Certainly Christ is a righteous Branch of David, fulfilling perfectly the will of God. Bound up with his person and sharing by trust in his righteousness, we are counted pure in the eyes of God. This is a righteous King who makes us righteous as well. And certainly too, Jesus Christ is just, in his life on this earth, bringing God's justice and order to the poor and oppressed, condemning the wicked, and setting right the relationships among human beings. Still today the risen Christ by his Spirit guides us in justice for all, and gives us the power to love one another.

But has this ancient promise been fully fulfilled? Do Judah and Jerusalem and, indeed, all the nations of the earth including ours, live in safety and security? Are our streets so safe now that we walk them at night? Are our children surrounded by a society of decency and peace? Can all of us enjoy an abundant life, free of violence and wrong, fear and upheaval? Or do the wicked still prowl through our society and world, and are countless millions still faced with the threat of death? Obviously, this promise in our text of safety and security has not yet fully been realized. The fulfillment of the total promise still awaits its time "in the days that are coming," when God brings it all to pass.

But remember! God is a promise-keeper. He began to fulfill this promise by sending us his own Son in the birth of that babe of Bethlehem. He has always kept his word in the past; the whole

13

history of Israel testifies to that faithfulness. So we now know that God will also keep his word — his full word — in the future.

The evil and violence, the sin and suffering that surround us on every side are not the last word. On this first Sunday of Advent, the church not only looks back to the birth of Christ, but it also looks forward to Christ's Second Coming, when he will come to set up his kingdom. Then in fact, safety and security and blessed life will be present for all people, and God will rule over all. God is a promise-keeper whose word will come to pass.

Second Sunday in Advent

Malachi 3:1-4

If we read the Old Testament in tandem with the New Testament, we sometimes have to employ a double focus. Verse 1 of our passage promises that God will send a messenger ahead to prepare the way of his coming. And that is certainly true when we look toward Christmas. God gives all sorts of preparatory signs before Jesus Christ is born in Bethlehem. An angel choir announces to shepherds that the one born is the Savior of the world. A rising and leading star alerts Mesopotamian astrologists to the fact that a special king has been born. Indeed, the whole Old Testament testifies to God's centuries of working toward the birth of his Son and centuries of Israel's longing for that saving Ruler.

Then, before God begins his ministry to his people and to the world in the person of his Son Jesus Christ, he sends the messenger, John the Baptist, to prepare the way. "I baptize you with water," that prophet preaches, "but he who is mightier than I is coming, the thong of whose sandals I am not worthy to untie; he will baptize you with the Holy Spirit and with fire" (Luke 3:16). Thus, the Gospels see in the person of the Baptist the fulfillment of the first line of our Malachi text.

Then we have to employ another focus, however, when we read the rest of this Malachi passage. After God sends his messenger to prepare his way, he will suddenly appear in his temple to judge and save his people. And that will be God's final, decisive coming — his Day of the Lord, the scriptures call it — when God appears to judge the earth and to set up his kingdom over all the world. At that time, evil-doers will be condemned and sentenced to death, but the righteous will be saved and exalted. Therefore, asks Malachi, "Who can endure the day of his coming, and who can stand when he appears?" (v. 2).

15

Can you? Can I? If we stand before the judgment seat of Almighty God, can our lives stand up to his scrutiny — the searching examination of the One who knows when we sit down and when we rise, and who discerns our every thought from afar (Psalm 139)? Have we always loved our God and our neighbor? Have we obeyed his commands and shown mercy to the poor and helpless and been faithful in our trust, even when we were suffering or in difficulty, or better still, even when everything was going right with us? Have we had no other gods beside the Lord? Or have we tried to be our own gods and goddesses and attempted to run our own lives, forgetful of our Creator and Redeemer?

Almighty God comes to judge the earth, proclaims Malachi along with the Psalmists (cf. Psalm 96:13; 98:9, *et al*) and other prophets. And if we ask, "How can that be?" the New Testament replies that the judgment will take place in the Second Coming of Jesus Christ. Then the Day of the Lord Christ will be at hand, and the Lord of the church will be our Judge. The Apostle Paul therefore prayed constantly that his churches would be found pure and blameless through faith "in the day of Christ" (Philippians 1:6, 10; 1 Corinthians 1:8; 1 Thessalonians 5:24), and Jesus repeatedly told us to "Watch!" and to be prepared, for we do not know when that hour will come (Mark 13; Matthew 24; Luke 21).

Our passage in Malachi states that God will send his messenger before the Day, and Malachi 4:5 identifies the messenger as Elijah. That encourages us to think that maybe we will have time to prepare ourselves before the last judgment. But, warns Jesus in the Gospels (Matthew 11:14; 17:11-12; Mark 9:13), Elijah has already come in the person of John the Baptist. The warning has been given. The preparing messenger has been sent. Now Christ can come again at any hour — maybe this afternoon, or tomorrow, or perhaps not for years. So the admonition simply is, "Watch!"

G. Campbell Morgan, a great preacher of the past generation, once wrote that here is the test of true faith and character. Can we gladly say, "Come, Lord Jesus. Yea, quickly come!" Are we ready eagerly to welcome Christ and to stand before his burning love? Or would we like to put off the coming of the kingdom, with its last judgment, indefinitely?

16

There is a hopeful note, however, in our Malachi passage. The prophet proclaims that when God comes in judgment, he will subject us to his refiner's fire and his cleansing fuller's soap. A refiner was one who sat before his bubbling cauldron full of ore and boiled out all of the impurities, until there was left pure gold or silver. A fuller bleached out spots from cloth, using strong soap made from lye, until the cloth was pure white and free from blemishes. Is that not what our Lord does in our lives also? Refining us by the little judgments of every day — troubling us, prodding us, sometimes pounding us, but always working to purify us, until we learn to rely totally on him and put behind our attempts to save ourselves.

We have the stereotype that God is with us only in peaceful and beautiful moments. But the scriptures tell us otherwise. God is present and at work in our lives also when we are suffering the fires of affliction. For example, we think that God is present only in a happy marriage. The truth is that he may be most present in an unhappy marriage — troubling, upsetting, shoving, trying to get us to turn around and to walk in his ways of forgiveness and healing.

Israel heard from Malachi that God was purifying her by the afflictions that she was suffering. So too God may be purifying us by the fires of his daily judgments and the cleansing lye of the troubles he brings upon us. But his aim is always that of love — to rid us of our sin. "Behold, the Lamb of God, who takes away the sin of the world," said John the Baptist of Jesus (John 1:29). Our Lord by his Spirit at work in our lives and world is taking away — taking away the sin that will make us unable to endure the coming of the Day of the Lord. By his action as the Refiner of our lives, God in Christ is able to keep us from falling and to present us without blemish before the presence of his glory with rejoicing (Jude 24).

Third Sunday in Advent

Zephaniah 2:14-20

Can we believe that God is carrying on a war against all sinners? He is, of course, according to the scriptures. Jeremiah gives us pictures of God attacking his sinful people in the form of that mysterious Foe from the North (Jeremiah chapters 4-6). Ezekiel declares that there is a breach in our wall of defense, caused by our sin, and that the role of a true prophet is to go up into that breach and by sacrifice and intercession, turn aside God's attack (Ezekiel 13:5). Earlier in Zephaniah, the prophet portrays the Day of the Lord when God the Warrior attacks all the sinful inhabitants of earth (Zephaniah 1:14-18). And in the New Testament, we are told that Christ is "destroying every rule and every authority and power. For he must reign until he has put all his enemies under his feet. The last enemy to be destroyed is death" (1 Corinthians 15:24-26). God hates sin, according to the scriptures, and he wars against every sinner.

To announce salvation to Israel therefore, Second Isaiah declares to her that "her warfare is ended" (Isaiah 40:2), that is, her warfare with God. And so too here in our Zephaniah text, the battle has been stilled, because God has cast out all of his enemies and left for himself a faithful and humble remnant (Zephaniah 3:11-13). The fourth line of verse 17 reads in the Hebrew, "He will hold his peace in his love," and the reference is to the war cry of God in 1:14. No longer does he shout as he enters into battle with his foes. The shouts and clang of battle have been stilled and there is peace, because God has defeated his enemies.

That is a picture of the future in Zephaniah, a time that will come "on that day" (v. 16). That phrase is found in most of the prophetic writings, and it always refers to an indefinite time in God's future, when he completes his work on earth and brings in his universal rule.

Further, says the Hebrew text of 17b, on that day God will be in the midst of his people, "a Mighty Man to save." No longer will he come to us in war, but his presence with us will be as a God of salvation, as a God of peace, who resides in the midst of his faithful folk.

Surely that is a cause of the rejoicing for which our text calls in 3:14. No longer will God be against us, but we will have peace with God — peace that passes all understanding and that the world can neither give nor ever take away. That is a cause for singing and rejoicing and exulting, because we are totally dependent on God. Zephaniah 1:12 quotes those people who say that God does nothing, but to the contrary, our very lives are in God's hands.

God is our Creator who breathed the breath of life into our nostrils in the first place, and who now sustains the regular pumping of our lungs in and out. God is the Maker who set the creation into order and who now sustains its every process by his faithfulness. Were he to leave the universe alone, it would collapse into chaos. God is he who gives us all the good gifts of life, of food and clothing, teaches Jesus, and even of our ability to have children and our families, adds Hosea (9:11-14). God is the Lord of love, who accompanies us daily, who constantly forgives us and guides us and strengthens us on our way. He keeps us from falling into temptation and constantly points out the way to life abundant. He draws near to us when we are in distress, and carries us in his everlasting arms. When we rely on his loving action in our lives, he sometimes gives us the power to soar up on wings like eagles and to run and not be weary. But always he gives us the ability to walk steadfastly forward, day by day. In his loving action, we find our security, and in his promises we have our hope for the future, knowing that nothing in all creation and not even death can separate us from the love he has for us in Jesus Christ our Lord. Yes, for all of these reasons, we rejoice and exult because God is present in our midst in peace, coming to us not as an enemy but as our everlastingly faithful Friend.

Not only do we rejoice over God's peaceful presence in our midst, however. Our text from Zephaniah also tells us that the Lord rejoices over us, celebrating because he can be in our company.

That is an almost unimaginable thought that Zephaniah gives us in verse 17 — that God exults and sings because he can be with us. Can you imagine that? The God who rules the universe is glad that he can be with you! The King of all the ages is made happy by his fellowship with us! Us! You and me, little incidents in the span of time, a cause for the eternal God to rejoice!

Could it be that is what God has wanted all along? That he created us in the first place for no reason at all except that his love produced us? And that he has desired nothing else except to make us into his people — a faithful people with whom he could enter into covenant fellowship; a trusting people to whom he could pour out good gifts; a loving people who would answer to his love with our own love for him?

When we look at the Son of God in the New Testament we find that all that is true. For Christ is the one who has given us peace with God, isn't he? He is the one who has defeated our enemies, our sin and death. By his death on the cross and his resurrection, he has given us back our lives, stilled God's warfare against us and made us new creatures. Christ is now the Son of God who dwells in our midst, in whom we find our joy and sure hope for the future.

To be sure, the full promise of this Zephaniah text awaits its fulfillment. We still flirt with sin every day and cause our Lord to grieve rather than to rejoice. We forget that he has conquered sin and that we could be rid of it. We still fear our death and the death of those whom we love, forgetting that the Lord Christ has conquered death and that in faith we can share his eternity. The remnants of evil still haunt our world, and many do not rejoice. Many even do not welcome the presence of Jesus Christ in their midst.

But the full promise comes, good Christians. It surely comes. Zephaniah gives us a picture of what that time will be like, and Jesus Christ has guaranteed its coming. So already, now, in this interim time, we can share in the gladness, knowing that in the Kingdom of God, this is the joy that lies out there ahead of us.

Fourth Sunday in Advent

Micah 5:2-5a

In the prophecies of Second Isaiah, the Lord God declares, "My thoughts are not your thoughts, neither are your ways my ways" (Isaiah 55:8), and how true that is of the God to whom the Bible witnesses! In our society, we adulate those whom we think are successful or talented or distinguished in some way. Many teenagers look up to a famous sports figure and try to imitate him on their own playing fields. Many viewers tune into the television program that interviews someone who is famous and rich. Fan clubs gather around Hollywood stars, and the faces of the so-called "beautiful people" look out at us from every magazine cover. Even, more soberly, the rich executive, the famous singer, the accomplished writer command our respect and attention. We look up to those whom we believe "have it made."

The God of the scriptures does not seem to take notice of our worldly standards, however. For a judge to lead his people in battle God chooses a man from the weakest tribe in Manasseh (Judges 6:15). For the first king of Israel he selects a Benjamite from the smallest tribe in Israel and from the humblest family in that tribe (1 Samuel 9:21). In our time, God picks out a black preacher from Georgia to lead a civil rights revolution. And he anoints a small and humble nun in India to teach the world what love and mercy mean. God chooses seemingly insignificant people to work his will in the world. As Paul wrote to the Christians in Corinth, "... not many of you were wise according to worldly standards, not many were powerful, not many were of noble birth" (1 Corinthians 1:26).

So it is too with God's future Messiah, according to our passage in Micah. That chosen Ruler of the world will come from the smallest clan within the tribe of Judah. To be sure, he will be from the line of David. He will come from Bethlehem Ephrathah, and

23

because David was the son of Jesse, "an Ephrathite of Bethlehem in Judah" (1 Samuel 17:12), the future Messiah will have a davidic heritage. But, as we know, he will be a lowly man, born in a cattle stall, raised up in a carpenter shop, and condemned to death as a criminal. Perhaps our evaluations of people in our society have nothing to do with God's thoughts and ways.

There is always a mystery surrounding the way God works in this world of ours, and that is certainly true of this messianic promise in Micah. We would like to categorize our Savior, to pin him down to a definite definition, to be able to say clearly and boldly just exactly who and what he is. But we cannot do that with this promised Messiah. His "origin is of old," says our text, "from ancient of days" and that latter phrase is used of God in the Book of Daniel (Daniel 7:9, 13, 22). The promised Messiah, Micah is telling us, will come not just from a small clan in Judah. He will also have his origin in God, and his birth will have been planned by God a long time ago. This ruler of the world, whom God will send to save his world, will be a man and yet more than a man, come from Judah but also from God.

So it is that when the early church wanted to tell who Jesus Christ is, in A.D. 451, it formulated what is known as the Creed of Chalcedon, to which the church has agreed ever since. "We, then ... all with one consent, teach men to confess one and the same Son, our Lord Jesus Christ, the same perfect in Godhead and also perfect in manhood; truly God and truly man ... Only begotten, in two natures, inconfusedly, unchangeably, indivisibly, inseparably...." Our Messiah, as Micah promises, is both God and man, both divine and human.

The God of the Bible not only does things in his own way, however. He also does them at his own time. We think sometimes that God should do some particular act right now, or at a time that we choose. The Judeans undoubtedly wanted God to save them in the eighth to sixth centuries B.C. But verse 3 of our text tells them that first they would have to go through the humiliation of their king in 597 B.C. and the deprivations of the Babylonian exile in 587 B.C. and following. The Messiah would not immediately appear on the scene. First, Israel had a chastening for her sins and a discipline to undergo, as we do also so often before we know our Savior to be with us. God prepares our hearts in many different ways before we are ready to receive him.

But the Messiah will come, Micah promises — that anointed one of the house of David, sent from God, raised up from the people, to do away with evil-doers and to bring to the faithful a realm of justice and righteousness, of peace and security and wholeness (cf. Micah 4:1-4).

The promised Messiah will "stand," said the prophet. That is, his reign will be forever. Despite all of the opposition to his rule; despite the fact that he will be "despised and rejected by men" (Isaiah 53:3); even if he should not be at all what anyone expects; indeed, even if we condemn him to death and hang him on a cross, his kingship shall be forever, and his rule shall never be defeated.

And what will the Messiah do? He will be a shepherd to us. "Shepherd" is another name for "king" in the Bible. But he will be a loving King, a Shepherd who feeds his flock. That is, he will provide us with the necessities of life and guide us in the right paths and protect us from all harm (cf. Psalm 23). Under his protecting rule, we will know peace in our lives, though all the world be in an uproar. We will know ourselves forgiven and accepted into his flock, our past sin and guilt done away by his mercy and renewal of us. We will find ourselves part of a new flock, of a new people, who trust in the Shepherd's rule. And we will find that nothing can separate us from the Shepherd's love for us.

All this will come to pass, says Micah, because the Shepherd will be given God's power, and all the wondrous acts that the Shepherd does will glorify his majestic Father God.

The Messiah will come — and he has come in the person of our Lord Jesus Christ — not for our sakes alone, however. Micah says that the name of the Messiah will be great in all the earth. In short, the Messiah's rule will extend over all people in his everlasting kingdom. This Son of God and son of man comes not just to bring us salvation. God gave his Son because he loves the whole wide world. And there shall come a time, Micah is saying, when our Lord will be known to all, and when his forgiven and saved people shall cover the face of the earth. To that promise given us by Micah, and to the beginning of its fulfillment in the birth of Christ, all of us, with all the faithful, can say, "Amen," at this Christmastime.

Christmas Eve Day

Isaiah 9:2-7

Darkness and light. The Bible constantly speaks of those two conditions. Genesis tells us that before God created the world, it was nothing but a stormy chaos engulfed in darkness. Exodus says that one of the plagues that God visited on the Egyptians was a plague of darkness, while all the Israelite slaves had light where they dwelt. Amos talks about the final day of judgment that will be a time of darkness and not light. At the crucifixion of Jesus, darkness covered the whole land from noon until the middle of the afternoon. And the author of Ephesians writes that those of faith are waging a war against sin that is a battle against the world rulers of this present darkness. Darkness is connected with evil and chaos and death in the Bible's metaphors, and say the scriptures, the only one who can dispel it is God.

So it is that our text from Isaiah is a promise that the people who walk in darkness will be given a great light by God. When the prophet Isaiah first pronounced that promise, it was directed to the Israelite regions of Zebulon and Naphtali, on the western side of the sea of Galilee in northern Israel (see v. 1). In 735 B.C., those tribes and in fact all of the region of northern Israel had been conquered by the Assyrian Empire. But, proclaimed Isaiah, God will raise up a new davidic king — an anointed one, a *mashiah* in the Hebrew, which we translate as Messiah. And that king, that Messiah, would free northern Israel and restore the far-flung boundaries of the davidic empire.

That's why our text talks about the rod of the oppressor being broken and the battle equipment of warriors being burned. The new davidic Messiah will bring in a realm of everlasting peace and justice and righteousness. No longer will the people be subjected to a foreign conqueror, because the Messiah's reign will be established forever. That was just a future promise given to Israel.

27

The writer of the Gospel according to Matthew said that promise had been fulfilled, however. After the death of John the Baptist, when Jesus withdrew into Galilee and began his ministry there in the regions of Zebulon and Naphtali, Matthew said Jesus was the one from God who was bringing light to a people who were walking in darkness (Matthew 4:15-16), and not just to that people, but to all people. On this Christmas Eve, with its candles and lights illumining the darkness, Jesus Christ brings us light.

Can that be said of you, that Christ brings you light? Certainly we all have our dark times, don't we? When the dailiness of life has got us down, and we just slog along in the same routine, and when we stop to think about it, there seems to be no point to it all. Then the future seems very dark, a tunnel with no light at the end.

Or darkness surrounds us when the anguish of a broken relationship crowds in on us, when hurts and fears and wounded pride all get bound up in a bundle of misery. Darkness comes when our own wrongdoing gnaws away at our innards, and regret hangs heavy in our thoughts. Darkness dims every dawn when illness wastes us, and it hurts to get out of bed. Darkness can be our daily companion when a loved one has died, and there seems to be no one to fill the void. Indeed, darkness far too often is the condition of our humanity. As one woman put it, "Life is tough. You're born, you suffer, and then you die." And that's all there is — the life, the pain and the suffering, and then the everlasting dark. But, says our text, to all of us who walk in darkness a great light is given. And, affirms the whole New Testament, his name is Jesus Christ — the babe born in the city of David, our long awaited anointed King, our Messiah.

How is it that he brings light into our lives? Our text from Isaiah furnishes us the answer. He is the Wonderful Counselor, the one who listens to all of our fears and trouble, poured out in our prayers from the midst of darkness. Christ listens to us and knows our hearts and sees our afflictions. He is not one who is unable to sympathize with our weaknesses, but rather one who has been tempted and troubled and has suffered in all the ways we have. And so he can guide us with his merciful directions in his teachings and point the way we are to walk. He told us once that he has given us all his commandments, that his joy may be in us, and that our joy may be full (John 15:11). Following his counsel is the way out of darkness into light.

Isaiah says our Messiah is also Mighty God — God incarnate come to earth to save and deliver us from evil. Not that everything will come up roses if we trust his working in our lives. But Christ acts with the power of that God who conquered creation's chaos, that God who could command the darkness and light at the time of the exodus, that God who defeated the darkness of death with the glories of Easter morn. It takes a God of might to overcome the dark evil in our world. But Jesus Christ is that Mighty God, who shines in the dark, and whose light the darkness can never extinguish.

Then too our Messiah, Isaiah foretold, is an Everlasting Father, exercising the mercy, the tenderness, the love of his Father on this earth. No matter how insignificant we may be, no matter what our station and status in life, no matter whether we be rich or poor, this Messiah gathers us all into his loving arms and lavishes on us a love that excels all other loves. Tenderness, mercy, understanding, forgiveness — our Messiah brings them all.

He also brings to us peace on earth, because he is the Prince of Peace; by such a title Isaiah characterized our Messiah. And do you remember his words? "Peace I leave with you," he said, "my peace I give to you; not as the world gives do I give to you" (John 14:17), but it is a peace passing all understanding. Indeed, friends, Christ brings a peace that will finally engulf this war-torn world, for his will be that universal reign, promised our text. There will come a day, say the scriptures, when every implement of war will be destroyed from the earth, God will be all in all, and we will know that blessed realm of which the Psalmist sings.

> *Steadfast love and faithfulness will meet;*
> *righteousness and peace will kiss each other.*
> *Faithfulness will spring up from the ground.*
> *and righteousness will look down from the sky.*
> Psalm 85:10-11

The light has come, good Christian friends, to all of us who walk in darkness.

Christmas Day

Isaiah 52:7-10

In biblical times, when a king was crowned in Israel, two acts took place. First, the king was crowned in the temple and presented with something that was called the "testimony" (2 Kings 11:12; 2 Chronicles 23:11). The testimony was probably some sort of document embodying the basic terms of the Lord's covenant with the house of David. As such, it was the legitimization of the king's rule by God. Second, the king was then led to his palace, he ascended his throne, and the beginning of his rule was proclaimed. At this point, messengers were dispatched throughout the land with the joyous cry, "So and so has become king" (cf. 2 Samuel 15:10; 2 Kings 9:13).

The coronation of a king was an occasion for great rejoicing among the people, because it meant that God had begun a new course with his people that might result in blessings poured out upon the populace. For example, when Solomon was crowned king over Israel, 1 Kings 1:40 tells us that "all the people went up after him, playing on pipes, and rejoicing with great joy, so that the earth was split by their noise." The hope of the people was that the new king would be a righteous king who would make the people righteous in God's sight and thus secure his favor toward them.

It is this custom that forms the background of Second Isaiah's hymn of joy in our text. The messengers have been sent out to announce the beginning of the reign of a new king over Israel. Israel languishes in Babylonian exile, but there is good news and hope for the future. Thus, "how beautiful upon the mountains are the feet" of those messengers. But the message that they bring to the despondent exiles is not that a new human king has ascended the throne. Rather, the messengers' joyful good news is that "your God reigns." God is their king. God reigns over all. God's is the kingdom and the power and the glory.

31

Here for the first time we have a picture of an evangel, of a bearer of good news, that is, of the bearer of the gospel, which means good news. And the good news that the evangels proclaim is that God is king.

Such too is the message of this Christmas day — that the Son of God has been born and that he is not only the King of the Jews, as even later on Pontius Pilate must confess (cf. John 19:21-22), but that he is also our King and King of the universe, who reigns over all. Christ the Messiah, Jesus Christ the anointed Son of God, is in charge. He rules over our lives and world.

I wonder if we grasp that. On the face of it, it seems like a dozen other influences rule over us and determine our lives these days: all of those schedules with their tyrannical deadlines that we feel ourselves obligated to meet; the demands of home and family, of job and calling that always hang over us; perhaps even the stereotypes of race or sex or economic status that others impose upon us. Or we might even say that in our society, the so-called experts run our lives. The nutrition experts tell us what to eat, so we won't develop cancer. The psychology experts tell us how to raise our children, or how to avoid stress and burnout. The fashion experts dictate what we wear, the sex experts invade our bedroom lives, and from every television screen our thought is guided and influenced. In the face of all of that can we truly say that our God reigns in his Son Jesus Christ?

But he does, you see. Whether we acknowledge it or not, whether we see the evidences of his rule or not, God is at work in your life and mine, holding them in his loving hand. Every moment he watches over us, and accompanies our steps, and sees our future. And he plans that future, working, prodding, guiding, weeping and judging and forgiving, all in order that we may have life and have it more abundantly.

I remember so vividly the day the young woman sat in my office, tears of hurt and disappointment coursing down her cheeks. The man she had thought she was going to marry had turned his back on her and left. I think we all have some kind of devastating moments like that, do we not, when a love fails us, or a job offer falls through, or a plan for the future that we so cherished goes awry? And in those moments, our scripture tells us, we are nevertheless being guided. God has a planned future for us. God rules our life.

We know that because Jesus Christ has been born. If ever a life seemed to end in shattered dreams and futility, it was his — his mission of love and healing and teaching come to naught but the thirst and pain and blood of a cross; denied by his inner circle, deserted by those he had called his friends. But God ruled his life; God was in charge. And so Golgotha gave way to Easter morn and that which had seemed futility turned into God's resurrection victory for us all. A cross which had been a symbol of death became God's way to life eternal.

I wonder if we can remember that when the futility and suffering and daily disappointments of life walk in our front door and sit down in our living rooms. Can we remember that God in Christ rules our lives and has a future for us all? Can we recall it when we worry about our children, and can we trust that God nevertheless watches over them every moment and guides and plans their destinies? Will we think of it when we cannot sleep at night, and remember that God never slumbers nor sleeps? Can we trust in the good sovereignty of God when pain seems to rule, or when we weep beside a fresh-dug grave? And yes, can we even believe it is so if this Christmastime is not filled with joy for some of us? God is in charge. God rules your life and mine.

Indeed, I wonder if we can remember that good news when we watch the tortured progress of nations. Few decades have seen the upheavals in international affairs that we have witnessed in the last few years, and all of it leaves us wondering just what is going to happen next. But who among those Israelite exiles in Babylonia would have thought that the Babyonian Empire would fall to Persia, and that Cyrus, king of Persia, would allow them to return to their homeland? God rules the life of nations, Second Isaiah proclaimed, and the captive Jews found themselves redeemed from exile, as you and I have been redeemed, delivered from the bondage of sin and the finality of the grave.

Is that not proof of it, dear friends? That God is in charge of our world and lives? He redeemed us from sin and death, and he will redeem our world. And so we too can hear the good news of this day, the gospel of everlasting joy. There is born in the city of David a Savior who is Christ the Lord — Christ, the Messiah, the king, the Word of God made flesh. And all the earth can break forth into singing and declare, "Our God reigns!"

First Sunday after Christmas

1 Samuel 2:18-20, 26

There are times in the life of the world or of a nation when one individual changes the whole course of history. Perhaps we might say that such a change occurred when the Emperor Constantine declared Christianity to be the official religion of the Roman Empire. Certainly we could agree that Martin Luther introduced an entirely new era when his actions initiated the Protestant reformation. And we might say that Mahatma Gandhi began the fall of the British Empire, or that Gorbachev began the dissolution of Soviet communism. Great sea changes in world history cluster around some individual.

The same is no less true in the biblical history. When Moses gave up his life as a common shepherd and went back to Egypt to demand that Pharaoh Rameses II let the enslaved Hebrews go, a new nation was born. When Elijah the prophet rose up in the tenth century B.C., to begin a prophetic revolution against Canaanite idolatry, a whole royal dynasty was toppled. And when Jesus of Nazareth was born in Bethlehem and died on a cross and was raised, time was split forever into B.C. (before Christ) and A.D. (*anno Domini*), the year of our Lord.

In that biblical history, however, was also another figure — that of Samuel, of whose boyhood we heard in our text. Samuel's mother had been barren and desperately wanted a son, and she vowed to the Lord that if the Lord would give her a son, she would dedicate the child to God's service in the sanctuary. So we find the boy Samuel "ministering before the Lord," says verse 18 in our text, helping the aged priest Eli with his duties at Israel's central sanctuary of Shiloh.

We must not think that Samuel's parents had abandoned him. Every year when his mother Hannah and his father Elkanah made a pilgrimage to Shiloh to worship the Lord, Hannah took along a new robe that she had made to give to the growing boy. Always Samuel was in her thoughts, as she stitched and embroidered that special robe. And every year she lovingly garbed her son anew.

But Samuel is a special child, dedicated to God from the beginning, growing up in the sanctuary of God, serving in the worship of the Lord, learning the traditions of Israel's faith from his childhood on. Indeed, the figure of Samuel marks a turning point in Israel's history.

After their settlement in Canaan, Israel had formed a loose confederation of twelve tribes, centered around a central sanctuary that was located first at Shechem and then Gilgal and finally Shiloh. At that central sanctuary was the ark of the covenant, which was thought of as the base of the throne of the invisible God, who was enthroned above it. Thus, God was present in the midst of his people, and every year, the Israelites assembled at Shiloh to worship the Lord and to renew their covenant with him. Eli and his sons served as Levitical priests at the sanctuary, while the leadership of the tribes was in the hands of those whom we call Judges.

As we read the story of Samuel, however, it becomes clear that Eli is aged and inept, while his priestly sons are corrupt. And so as he is wont to do, God raises up a new figure to serve not only as priest but also as judge and prophet for Israel. God raises up Samuel, and Samuel is the transition figure between the time of the tribal federation in Israel and the beginning of the monarchy under Saul.

In our text, Samuel is already clothed with the priestly ephod. And as his story progresses he becomes the prophet who mediates the word of the Lord to Israel, as well as the leader who acts as judge over the people. Samuel combines in his person the offices of priest, prophet, and judge. It is no wonder therefore that the words said of Samuel in verse 26 are also the words used to describe the boy Jesus in Luke 2:52. Samuel grows in stature and in favor with God and with the people, just as Jesus grows, who is to become the final Prophet, Priest, and King over all. Samuel is understood as a forerunner, as a foreshadowing of our Lord, as a decisive figure in the history of God's chosen people. God works through centuries to fulfill his plan of salvation.

Samuel grew in stature, which simply means he grew taller, as every child grows taller. We sometimes get the impression that characters in the Bible are not real people. But Samuel was a real human boy, as Jesus was a real human boy. They both grew in height, and Samuel's mother had to keep making a new robe for him every year. As we know all too well, children have a way of growing out of their clothes.

But Samuel also grew in favor with the Lord, as is said also of Jesus, and I wonder if that is a word, not only about Samuel and Jesus, but also about us. Do you, year by year, grow in favor with the Lord?

There is a doctrine in the Christian Church that our age has almost forgotten. It is called the doctrine of sanctification, and what it signifies is our continual growth in goodness and obedience and trust in God. The scriptures tell us that the Christian life is never a static state of being. It is a growth, a progress toward maturity in Christ. We are to grow up into mature manhood or womanhood, says the letter to the Ephesians, up into the measure of the fullness of the stature of Christ. In other words, every day and every year, we are to become more like Jesus. In fact, the Apostle Paul tells us that is what God is trying to do in our lives. By the work of the Spirit, Paul tells the Corinthians, God is changing us into the likeness of Christ, from one degree of glory to the next (2 Corinthians 3:18).

We rarely think about that. In our society, who wants to be good anymore? We have all sorts of goals. We want to be successful or slim or self-assertive or rich or beautiful, but good? Do you want to be good? Do you want to be a woman of God or a man of God? Is that the image that you want other people to have of you? Do you want to be known for your love of your neighbors and for your love of God?

Yes, deep down inside of us, we all want that. We all want to be like Jesus. We sing, "Lord, I want to be like Jesus, in'a my heart, in'a my heart." And from our text, we could add, "Lord, I want to be like Samuel." But that takes work, doesn't it? It takes what we call Christian discipline. Growing up into the measure of the fullness of the stature of Christ, or even of Samuel, is not a matter of just floating down the stream of grace. No. It's a matter of daily and consistent prayer, a matter of careful study of the scripture, a matter of regular worship and of willful practice and service in our everyday lives. Growing up into Christian maturity is a matter of getting out of bed every morning and praying, "Lord, enable me by your Spirit to do your will this day and to grow in knowledge and love of you," and then bending mind and heart and strength and will to walk the Christian way.

Samuel grew in favor with the Lord. May we follow his example.

New Year's Day

Ecclesiastes 3:1-13

All of us know that there are proper times to do and say certain things. For example, if we are gardeners, we know that peas and lettuce should be planted in the early spring. If we are attending a funeral, we are aware of the fact that it is no time to laugh. If a family member is unreasonably angry with us and thinks we don't care for him at all, it may be the time to put our arms around him and assure him of our love.

Words and actions have their proper times, and that is part of the Wisdom teaching that comes to us from the book of Ecclesiastes. Especially, says Wisdom tradition, is there an appropriate time to keep silence or to say just the right word (v. 7; cf. Proverbs 15:23; 25:11). I think we all know of times when the right word said at the right time has lent enormous comfort to a troubled soul or even set someone's life on a better path. But we also know of times when someone has blurted out something at a party that never should have been said or a gossip has told a confidence that never should have been passed on. There is a time to speak, as our text says, and a time to keep silence.

Ecclesiastes is part of the body of Wisdom writings that is found in our Bible, primarily in the books of Job, Proverbs, some Psalms, and Ecclesiastes. But Wisdom sayings also are sprinkled throughout both Old and New Testaments. For example, Jesus uses an illustration from Wisdom teaching in Matthew 7:24-27.

The basic theological belief of Wisdom is that when God created the world, he established certain orders in both human life and in the natural world around us, customary ways in which both human beings and nature act. Those customary orders have been discovered by Wisdom teachers by careful observation, and the teachers have then set down in the Wisdom writings what they have learned of the orders. The wise person, therefore, is one who learns what Wisdom says and acts in accordance with the ordered ways

39

of nature and human society. Such a person finds life, says Wisdom. But the fool is one who refuses to learn the orders and defies them, acting contrary to them. Such a fool finds only death.

As an illustration of that, we might say that one of God's orders set into human marital life is life-long faithfulness to one's spouse. Such faithfulness can bring with it a good marriage, full of joy. But a fool ignores that and goes out and commits adultery, so that marital trust is destroyed, the unity of wife and husband is broken, and the marriage brings only trouble, ending in the death of the relationship.

As our text from Ecclesiastes 3 shows, one of the orders that God has set into his creation is also the order of time, not only the cycle of the seasons and days and months and years, but also the order of time into which our lives fit. The presupposition of Wisdom, therefore, is that all human activity is not successful and meaningful at every time, and if we do not know the proper time to do something, our activity can turn out badly.

There is, says our text, even a proper time to die. We age as we increase in years, though our youth-oriented culture tries to deny the process of aging. We all try to stay young-looking. So Hollywood stars and figures in public life have face-lifts, or we use hair coloring or makeup to cover gray hair and wrinkles. We all have known persons in their sixties who try vainly to look as if they were still forty. And they do, as Wisdom implies, appear to be fools. But the years go on, time's order is that of passing, and eventually we all confront our death.

Indeed, one of the wisest approaches we can take to our life is to know that we are going to die. "So teach us to number our days," sings the Psalmist, "that we may get a heart of wisdom" (Psalm 90:12). Then we realize that we are not gods and goddesses, but that we are mortal; that we are not the Creator but his creatures; and that there is an everlasting Love beyond the span of our years that holds our lives in his merciful hands.

The Lenten season always emphasizes that fact when it includes the ritual of marking our foreheads with ashes. We are told by the minister in that ritual, "Remember that you are dust." And what the rest of our passage in Ecclesiastes tells us as we begin this

40

new year is to make the most of our years. In the words of Ephesians, "Look carefully then how you walk, not as unwise persons but as wise, making the most of the time, because the days are evil" (Ephesians 5:15-16). We can live our lives joyfully in the service of God, or we can waste them on foolish and evil practices. One thing is certain, however: they will come to an end. And perhaps instead of trying vainly to prolong a life beyond the proper time to die, we should have the wisdom to know when that proper time is.

In the meantime, however, Ecclesiastes tells us to enjoy the good life that God has given us. In many ways, it is a grateful and joyful book. The writer of Ecclesiastes, who is called the Preacher, is thankful for the many gifts that God has lavished upon him, and he urges that same thankfulness upon his readers. He knows that all good things in life come from God, and that there is no joy apart from God (2:24-25). Therefore, he says, take the joy from life that God gives you (cf. 8:15; 9:7). If you are wealthy, enjoy your wealth; otherwise you are better dead (6:1-6). If you are married, enjoy your life with the wife whom you love (9:9). Appreciate the beauty of the earth (3:11), food and drink and prosperity (10:19; 9:7), and wise and proper government (10:16-17). But above all, enjoy the work that God has given you to do (2:24; 3:22; 5:18-20), as verse 13 of our text says, for the "night comes, when no one can work" (John 9:4), even death.

Ecclesiastes is also a humble book, however, and in verse 11 of our text, it sets forth the traditional Wisdom teaching that finally human beings cannot know everything. Above all, they cannot know all the ways of God. There is a mystery to God's working that human minds cannot plumb, and we have humbly to acknowledge that mystery by placing our lives fully in God's all-wise hands.

If we do that, if in gratitude we thank God for his many gifts and in humility submit ourselves to his kindly plan and working, we also know in the Christian faith something that the writer of Ecclesiastes does not know: that in the plan and love of God, death is not the end of all our enjoyment and work. Rather, through faith in Jesus Christ, our lives are taken up in resurrection, our good work is completed and made perfect, and we enter God's eternal kingdom for evermore.

41

Epiphany of Our Lord

Isaiah 60:1-6

This serves as the stated text for Epiphany in all three cycles of the lectionary. The preacher may therefore want to look at the expositions in Cycles A and B also.

The church has designated this text for the celebration of Epiphany Sunday, that Sunday when it announces the fact that the gospel is intended for all peoples throughout the world. Both accompanying stated texts emphasize that fact. In the story of the wise men, who symbolize the foreign nations, Matthew shows them coming to Bethlehem to worship the infant Jesus. In Ephesians, Paul's ministry to the gentile world is proclaimed.

Set in that context, this Isaiah passage takes on an interesting twist when it is applied to Jesus. When it speaks of "kings," verse 3, coming to the "light," the light is understood as Jesus, and verse 6 says that the foreigners will bring him gifts of "gold and frankincense." That of course calls the story from Matthew 2 to mind.

Originally, however, the unknown author of this passage intended it as a proclamation of salvation to post-exilic Israel in the last quarter of the sixth century B.C. Many of the Israelites have returned to Jerusalem from their exile in Babylonia, but Jerusalem lies still in ruins, and life is very hard. Thus, Jerusalem is pictured in this passage as a woman, mourning in the dust for her lost children and lost glory. She has been chastised for her continuing sin against the Lord, a judgment spelled out in the preceding chapters 56-59.

Now, however, God declares that he will nevertheless be present in the midst of his people in his "glory" (vv. 1, 2) to restore the life of his people and to make them honored among all the nations. The central thought is stated in verse 10: "In my wrath I smote you, but in my favor I have had mercy on you." Israel does not deserve such mercy, but nevertheless a loving God will shower it upon her.

As a result, Israel will shine with the reflected glory of her God who is present in her midst, and all nations will be gathered to her light. They will carry Israel's exiled children back to Jerusalem (v. 4) and bring with them abundant gifts to rebuild the temple and to supply its sacrifices (vv. 5-7). There will be camels bearing gifts from the desert tribes of Midian and Ephah; gold and frankincense from the Arabian trading center of Sheba; herds from Kedar and Nabaioth; silver and gold from the sea peoples; fine timber from the North. But all will be brought to pay homage, not to Israel, but to the Lord (vv. 6, 9). Because the peoples see that God has visited his people and saved them, all nations will be drawn to Israel's light, to worship that saving God. (The thought is the same as that found in Isaiah 52:13—53:12 and Zechariah 8:22-23.)

So to be true to the text, the preacher can apply this passage to Israel, as it was originally intended, or the preacher can take the text as a reference to Jesus, as in the tradition of the church. There is, however, another option that preserves the integrity of the text.

Suppose we read this passage as an address to the church, the new Israel in Jesus Christ. Certainly in many passages in the New Testament the church is conceived to be "the Israel of God" (Galatians 6:16), the "true circumcision" (Philippians 3:3), that has not replaced Israel but that has been joined to her (cf. Romans 11:17-24; Ephesians 2:11-22). Thus, that which was spoken to Israel by the prophet can be understood as spoken to us, the Christian Church. Read in such a manner, this Isaiah text then becomes a call to the church to be the church.

Certainly there is a lot of mourning taking place in our main-line churches these days. Our life is characterized by conflict, by loss of members, by confusion of theology, by insufficient resources. To that mournful condition, God through this prophet now addresses his word: "Arise, shine; for your light has come, and the glory of the Lord has risen upon you!"

What is that glory? It is the birth, life, death, and resurrection of Jesus Christ. As Paul writes, God "has shown in our hearts to give the light of the knowledge of the glory of God in the face of Christ" (2 Corinthians 4:6). God, in his glory, has come into our midst in the incarnated Person of his Son. Moreover, he has promised us that he remains with us always, even to the close of the age (Matthew 28:20). And he has assured us that nothing in all creation, not even death itself, will separate us from Christ's loving presence with us (Romans 8:38-39). We do not deserve that presence any more than Israel deserved God's presence with her in ruined Jerusalem. Nevertheless, Christ is Immanuel, God with us, in sheer mercy and love.

The role, the mission, of the church then is to reflect in its life the light of the glory of Christ, just as Israel was to reflect the light of God's presence with her. The church's words and proclamations are to point to Christ's work and to declare Christ's redemption. The church's actions are to mirror Christ's love and to imitate Christ's deeds of mercy. The church's worship is to be directed toward the glorification of Christ, praising him for all he has said and done for all peoples everywhere. In short, the life of the church is to reflect that of its Lord — his love, his sacrifice, his mercy, his goodness, his unstinting obedience of his Father. It is not the church that is to live, but Christ who is to live in it, so that when all peoples look at the church, they see instead Jesus Christ, still at work in his body, the church, to bring his salvation to all peoples.

If the church can carry out that God-given mission and truly be Christ's body and not its own, then indeed, all peoples everywhere will flow to it, as God says in our Isaiah passage that they would flow to Jerusalem. There, in a faithful church, the nations of the world may see that for which they have so longed — the reflected light of God's peace, of God's truth, of God's hope, of God's joyful salvation. Then there will be "good news" for all peoples and not the evil tidings that we read in our newspapers. If the church will truly be the church, it can spread the gospel to the whole wide world.

There are little groups here and there in the universal church who carry on such a mission now, so it is not an impossible dream. Such groups believe God's promises, given in the scriptures, and so they shine with the light of Christ among them. They do so, however, not by their own efforts, not by their own planning, not by their self-conceived programs, but by surrendering themselves wholly to the working of Christ in their midst. God's salvation of the world comes not from us, but from Jesus Christ working in us. It is not our light that is to shine forth, but the reflected light of God's glory in our Lord.

Baptism of Our Lord

Isaiah 43:1-7

The subject for this Sunday, as set forth in the accompanying New Testament texts, is baptism, the baptism of Jesus in Luke, and the baptism of the Samaritan disciples in Acts. Let us therefore use our Second Isaiah text also in relation to baptism, namely our baptisms. To be sure, the prophet originally directed these words to the Israelite exiles in Babylonian between 550 and 538 B.C., but they are also an excellent description of our relation to God in our baptisms into the church.

The words and especially the verbs to note in this text, which is technically called a "salvation oracle," are those that describe what God has done, is doing, or will do. God has "created," "formed," "redeemed," "called you by name" (v. 1). He is "with you" (vv. 2, 5). He is "your Savior" (v. 3). He considers you "precious" and "esteemed," and he "loves" you (v. 4). He will "gather you" from the four corners of the earth (vv. 5-6). He "created," "formed," and "made" everyone who is called by his name, for his glory (v. 7).

The focus of the text is entirely on God's action, but because his action is done in relation to us, because he is the God who is "with" us, everything said about God's deeds is important for us church members.

When we come to our baptisms, or when we present a child to be baptized, the first fact we are to remember is that God has "created" us. But that has been the most intimate sort of creation. God has "formed us," say verses 1 and 7, like a potter working with a lump of clay, shaping our bodies and organs and muscles in the wombs of our mothers. As Job says, "Thou didst clothe me with skin and flesh, and knit me together with bones and sinews" (Job 10:11). God intentionally created each one of us because he had a purpose for each one of us.

47

More than that, God also created the church. The Christian Church did not exist before God prefigured it in his covenant people Israel and then called it into being in Jesus Christ (cf. Matthew 16:18-19). We are a God-created and God-shaped people, who had no existence before God formed us as his church (cf. Ephesians 2:12-22). Only because of God's act, do we have this beloved community into which we are baptized, and apart from God in Jesus Christ there is no church.

That which binds us all together in this household of faith, however, is the fact that we have all been "redeemed" together. That is what we have in common — not blood, not soil, not economics or status. Rather, we share together the one fact that God has redeemed us all. He redeemed Israel out of Egypt, that is, he bought her back out of slavery, which is what redemption means (cf. Leviticus 25:47-49). And so too he redeemed each one of us out of slavery to sin and death, and he redeemed the person who is to be baptized. Long before our baptisms, long before any one of us had done anything to deserve it (cf. Romans 5:8), God redeemed us from sin and death by the cross and resurrection of Jesus Christ.

In our baptisms, therefore, the God who bought us back calls us by our names and claims us as his own. At every baptism the Christian name of the person is pronounced, and that person becomes God's child. No longer does the baptized person belong to the world. No, he or she belongs to God, and the promise is that nothing can snatch the baptized person out of the loving hand of God who has claimed her or him.

To be sure, evil may come and tribulations may abound in a baptized person's life. As our text says in verse 2, we may "walk through the fire" of trial and suffering, we may be almost overwhelmed by the "waters" of a chaotic and violent world. But God's word of consolation is sure: "I am with you." Therefore, we need have no fear (vv. 1, 5), for in Paul's words, "Neither death, nor life, nor angels, nor principalities, nor things present, nor things to come, nor powers, nor height, nor depth, nor anything in all creation, will be able to separate us" (Romans 8:38-39) from God who has claimed us as his own. Always "underneath are the everlasting arms" (Deuteronomy 33:27), and he holds us secure to all eternity.

God is the baptized persons' "Savior" in all circumstances. We are "precious" to God and "esteemed" by him. Indeed, he "loves" us. Other people may think we are unimportant or unworthy of notice. We may hold the most humble and insignificant position in our job or society, in some little forgotten corner of our land. But we are not unimportant to God. He sees us. He knows our needs. He numbers the very hairs of our heads, and knows even when we sit down and when we rise (Psalm 139:2). He hears our prayers, and indeed, his Son prays for us (cf. Romans 8:34).

Think of it! The Almighty Creator of heaven and earth, who ignited the sun and raised up the Rocky Mountains, who commands the stars and can direct the ways of nations, that Lord of all nature and human history watches each moment over us, his children, in love. He neither slumbers nor sleeps, but keeps us always in his mind and care, and daily he guides our steps in mercy, leading us lovingly toward his everlasting kingdom.

God in Christ has, in fact, as our text says, gathered his people from east and west, from north and from south. His baptized folk now form, as the hymn says, "one great fellowship of love throughout the whole wide earth." We enter by our baptisms into a universal church, made up of people of every race and clime. And the one to be baptized becomes a member not only of a local congregation, but of the one church of Jesus Christ that is found throughout the world.

God has "formed and made" us his people not simply for our sakes alone, however. As wondrous as his gifts are to all of his baptized folk, with our baptisms has come a task given each one of us. God has created us, says our text, for his "glory" (v. 7). In baptism, God has poured out the Spirit of Christ upon us, and now he desires that we use that power to glorify his name in all the earth. That is, we are to make the Lord God esteemed and honored, worshiped and loved by all people everywhere. We are given the task of so proclaiming Christ that every knee bows and every tongue confesses that he is their Lord also.

How do we carry out that awesome task? By telling what God has done in our lives, as Old and New Testament tell it, and by living our lives in the manner that shows that the good news of the gospel is true. We glorify God by showing and telling other people about the actions and words of the Lord. That is what Second Isaiah does in our text for the morning. And that is the task to which we, God's baptized people, are called.

Second Sunday after Epiphany

Isaiah 62:1-5

For those who like to preach from all three lectionary texts, the stated readings for this Sunday could cause a preacher great perplexity. How on earth do they all fit together? The Epistle lesson deals with the variety of gifts given by the Spirit to the church. The Gospel lesson recounts Jesus' first "sign" at the wedding at Cana, when the water turned into wine, became the symbol of his blood poured out for us all. Our Isaiah text concerns the eschatological future of Jerusalem. Other than the reference to a wedding in John and here in Isaiah, the texts seem to have nothing in common.

Actually all three texts can be used to speak of the church. Through years of tradition, the Christian Church has been identified with Jerusalem as the "Zion of God." "O Zion haste, thy mission high fulfilling," we sing. If we keep that traditional imagery, Isaiah 62:1-5 then may be used as a proclamation to the church, and the central thought of the passage is that the church will be given two new symbolic names: "Hephzibah," meaning "my (that is, God's) delight is in her," and "Beulah" meaning "married" (that is, to the Lord. This is the passage from which we get the phrase "Beulah land").

God will give us new names, but like the peoples in the story of the Tower of Babel, we in the church have always tried to "make a name for ourselves" (Genesis 11:4). To be sure, we call ourselves evangelicals or liberals, Presbyterians or Baptists, Methodists or Episcopalians, and so forth. But beyond that, we have always been concerned with our image. We want our church to be known as a mega-church or as a socially-active denomination in the U.S. And locally, we want others to acknowledge that we are the most successful church in town, or the friendliest. We point to our lively youth groups and our magnificent choirs, to the beauty of our sanctuary or to our historic past. We glorify our programs and our mission budget, all in the effort to show others that our congregation is preeminent and surely the one to which any sensible Christian would want to belong.

If we would identify with the Zion of Isaiah, however, perhaps we should ask ourselves if our names are really "Forsaken" and "Desolate" as the prophet says. Because we have so often tried to glorify ourselves and our own programs rather than God, is our name actually "Forsaken"? Have we forsaken our true mission of glorifying God? Have we loved ourselves more than we have loved God and neighbor? And have we followed our own plans rather than the plans that the Lord has for us?

If that is true, then perhaps are we also "Desolate," as the prophet announces? Do we really have a place in God's ongoing purpose? Is there any lasting, eternal meaning to the programs we are carrying out? Is what we are doing in our congregation designed to further God's plan for all people, to bring in his kingdom on earth even as it is in heaven? Or are we a little group whose work will disappear in the sands of time and finally be insignificant?

These are very hard questions for any congregation to face, but perhaps the Word of the Lord that comes to us this morning from Isaiah is intended to make us face the questions and to evaluate our church's life once again. Whom are we serving in this church, God or ourselves?

Our text from the Third Isaiah (chs. 56-66) is not intended to be an announcement of judgment, however. It is what is known as a "salvation oracle," and the ultimate message that it brings is not bad news but good.

Despite Judah's ongoing sin — and ours — despite the church's neglect of the things of God for the service of itself, God nevertheless plans for his people his bright future (note the reference to light in v. 1) and not the dark future that our faithlessness deserves. Always God's mercy breaks into the world to bring the fulfillment of his plan of love.

There will be deliverance and salvation for God's covenant people (v. 1), for Judah and for the church, and our lives will be shaped to be a thing of beauty in the hand of our God (v. 3), which is a beautiful metaphor for the loving care with which God our

King will claim us, God will so transform his church that it will be a delight to him (v. 4), a "bride" over which the divine "bridegroom" can rejoice (vv. 4-5). We in our sin cannot transform our own life as a church, but God can and will.

The language of God as the bridegroom and husband of his people is frequent in the scriptures. Already in earlier prophetic writings, Israel was spoken of as the bride of God (Jeremiah 2:2; Ezekiel 16:8; Hosea chs. 2-3). And our Lord took up that language in his teachings to refer to himself as the bridegroom (Mark 2:19-20 and parallels; Matthew 25:1, 5, 6, 10; cf. John 3:29; Ephesians 5:32). Thus, the Apostle Paul's hope for the church is that it will be presented as a pure bride to Christ (2 Corinthians 11:2), and the future vision of Revelation is that in the Kingdom of God, the church will come "down out of heaven from God, prepared as a bride adorned for her husband" (Revelation 21:2; cf. vv. 9, 17; 19:7), "without spot or wrinkle or any such thing" (Ephesians 5:27), holy and without blemish. In short, God will so work in the life of the church that he will purify us and deliver us from all sinful ways. We are not worthy to enter the Kingdom of Heaven, but in Christ, God will make us new, until we can be the people in whose midst he promises to dwell in delight forever (Revelation 21:3).

The prophet prays for that future salvation in our text. He says that he will never cease praying (v. 1) or give God rest until God "establishes Jerusalem and makes it a praise in the earth" (v. 7). Surely, for the same happy outcome for the church, we should pray also. Indeed, every time we pray the Lord's prayer, we utter that petition: "Thy kingdom come on earth even as it is in heaven." "Lord," we are saying in so many words, "purify thy church. Make us holy and whole, so that we are a delight to you. Transform us by your Spirit to be the church you intended us to be. Prepare us to be your Bride in the new Jerusalem of your kingdom." And perhaps if we earnestly, consistently pray that prayer, and mean it, we will open our lives more and more to God's transformation of us.

Third Sunday after Epiphany

Nehemiah 8:1-3, 5-6, 8-10

We live in a society in which right and wrong have become largely a matter of personal opinion. All individuals are seen as a law unto themselves, and what is right for one person is not necessarily right for anyone else. Indeed, if any person tries to impose their ethical standards on another, the response is usually defensive anger. "Don't try to impose your middle-class morality on me," goes the complaint. "I know what is right for me, and you have no business trying to meddle in my life!"

The result is that there is no common standard of conduct that governs our lives. The country is split into a multiplicity of little groups, each pursuing its own values and setting its own ethical agendas. Frequently there is conflict, each little group trying to gain power for its point of view and scorning the standards and lifestyles of other groups. Vainly, government and media and schools try to return to a basic set of "American values" or "family values," but relativity reigns, and everyone does his or her own thing. A sardonic statement at the end of the book of Judges could apply to our society: "In those days there was no king in Israel; everyone did what was right in his own eyes" (Judges 21:25).

In some sense, we might see that as the situation of the Israelites when they returned to Jerusalem in the sixth and fifth centuries B.C. after the Babylonian exile. Their religious traditions and knowledge of God's directions for their lives had been forgotten, and they were left with nothing but their own desires and wisdom to reconstruct their shattered community. A community that has forgotten its founding story and common ethic cannot be a community, however. It can only be a conglomeration of competing groups and interests, as our society often is, and apparently the people in post-exilic Jerusalem in the fifth century B.C. were wise enough to realize that.

According to our text in Nehemiah, the people of Jerusalem all gathered in a square of Jerusalem, and "they *told* Ezra the scribe to bring the book of the law of Moses which the Lord had given to Israel" (v. 1). They demanded to hear the Torah.

We would not want that, would we? If someone wanted to read us a story that contained commandments for our lives, we might quickly leave the scene. Our pious excuse, of course, would be that we are Christians who are saved by faith and not by some law. But the Jews in Ezra's time had a different understanding of the Torah than we have, and they wanted desperately to hear it.

What follows in our text is therefore a worship service in a square in Jerusalem. Ezra mounted a pulpit and when he opened the book of the Torah, all of the people stood and listened attentively. As Ezra read portions of the first five books of the Old Testament, Levitical priests standing beside Ezra translated the Hebrew words into Aramaic, the language of the day, and explained the meaning of the words to the people, so that they understood them. When the people heard laws that they had forgotten, statutes that they had not observed, explanations of the Word of God, they wept, not for sorrow at their sin, but for joy at hearing once again — and some of them for the first time — the directions of God for their community and individual lives. They not only heard commandments, however. From the Torah they heard the old, old traditions of how God had delivered them from slavery and entered into covenant with them. They were prompted to remember how God had led their forebears through the wilderness and given them the promised land. And through it all, they heard the voice of the Lord, guiding them, forgiving them, accompanying them in his law, and pointing out the way they were to walk as his people. To it all, they said, "Amen," and they wept for joy.

Now why? Why should a reading of commandments give us joy? We can understand how it would be good to review once again God's saving acts on our behalf, as they are told in the Pentateuch and the rest of the scriptures. But why should we rejoice over laws and commandments? Isn't that legalism?

No, it is not. The commandments that are given us in the Bible, such as the Ten Commandments, and all of the instructions that

Jesus and Paul and the other writers set down for us in the New Testament are expressions of God's love. You see, God has delivered us from slavery to sin and death, as he delivered Israel from Egypt. And in Jesus Christ, God has given us a new life. As Paul writes, "The old has passed away, behold, the new has come" (2 Corinthians 5:17) — all those sins and guilts of the past, all of our inabilities to do the good, all of our despairs and anxieties that we have gone through. Those are now done. God has forgiven us in Jesus Christ and lent us his Spirit that we may walk in newness of life and in the goodness that God intends.

Having redeemed us in Jesus Christ, however, God does not just let us stumble around in the dark, wondering what to do in this new life we have been granted and making up the rules as we go along. God does not desert us any more than he deserted post-exilic Israel. No. God continues to go with us and to guide us, and he does that by giving us commandments. God points the way, which is the basic meaning of "Torah." He says, "Here is the way to walk. Here is the way to abundant life. Walk in it, and so choose life."

God points the way to abundant life by means of his commandments, because he loves us and wants only good for us. Both Old Testament and New tell us that. In Deuteronomy 4:29, God yearns for his people's good: "Oh that they had such a mind as this always," he says, "to fear me and to keep all my commandments, that it might go well with them and with their children for ever!" God wants it to go well with us! God wants us to have good. Similarly, in the Gospel according to John, Jesus tells his disciples that if they keep his commandments, they will abide in his love (John 15:10) and then he adds, "These things I have spoken to you, that my joy may be in you, and that your joy may be full" (v. 11). The Lord wants us to have joy! And so he instructs us in the way to abide in fellowship with him and to have a joyful life.

That is what Israel knew when she heard Ezra read the Torah to her in that square in Jerusalem and wept tears of happiness — that following the Word of God was the way of joy and life. So her Psalmist could write that the Torah was more to be desired than gold and sweeter than the drippings of the honeycomb (Psalm 19:10). And every faithful Christian who walks in the way of Christ's commandments knows that sweetness and that treasure that come from walking in God's way and not in our own.

Fourth Sunday after Epiphany

Jeremiah 1:4-10

We modern-day Christians are not called to be prophets in the Old Testament sense of the term. We must remember that when preaching from this text. An Israelite prophet was one who had the ecstatic experience of standing "in the council (i.e., the heavenly court) of the Lord to perceive and to hear his word" (Jeremiah 23:18; cf. 1 Kings 22:13-23; Isaiah 40:1-8). He was then sent as a messenger of that council to tell where, when, and why God was at work in Israel's life. Old Testament prophets had new words from the Lord to proclaim, but we Christians believe that the Word of God has now been spoken and incarnated in its fullness in Jesus Christ, and we add nothing to that Word. Who can add anything to the cross and resurrection? Rather we simply spell out, expound, and explain the meaning of that full Word for our time.

Nevertheless, the God who called the youthful Jeremiah of Judah in 626 B.C. is also our God, and the revelation given in this text to the prophet at the beginning of his ministry can also be a witness to us of God's nature and purpose. Certainly the text centers on God. Six times the word "Lord" appears in the text.

Who is the God revealed through this call? First, he is a God of intimacy. There are no angelic mediators here, nor is Jeremiah overwhelmed with the vision of God's transcendent glory, as was Isaiah (ch. 6). Rather God himself fashioned Jeremiah in his mother's womb, like a potter working with a lump of clay (v. 5), as he has fashioned each one of us, and he knows Jeremiah and us through and through (cf. Psalm 139). Similarly, God himself reaches out his hand and touches the prophet's lips and puts his words in his mouth (v. 9).

Second, the God who calls Jeremiah is Lord of lords and King of kings. Jeremiah is called to be a prophet to "nations" and "kingdoms," and God can establish and build up those nations or pluck them up and break them down, verse 10. Like Jesus passing majestically through the midst of the lynch crowd in the Gospel lesson of Luke 4:21-30, God in Jeremiah is the Almighty Sovereign in control. Thus, Jeremiah calls God "Adonai" (v. 6), that is, "Master" or "Owner."

This mighty Lord calls an insignificant youth from the Benjamite town of Anathoth to be his messenger. Jeremiah, at the time of this call, is a young man of marriageable age, about eighteen years old, and there is nothing about him that qualifies him to be the Lord's prophet. He has never spoken in public in his life. Indeed, throughout his ministry he is terrified by his task and argues constantly against it. The God of the scriptures, it seems, calls those who are weak and foolish and despised in the world (1 Corinthians 26-27), in order that it may be seen that it is God's power that works through them and not their own.

God always equips his ministers and messengers and disciples for their tasks, however, providing his sufficiency where they have none. To Jeremiah's "I do not know," the Lord replies, "I knew you." To Jeremiah's "I am only a youth," God answers, "I am with you," and then he gives Jeremiah the words he is to speak. As Paul says, God's grace is sufficient for us, and his power is made perfect in our weakness (2 Corinthians 12:9).

The reason for God's call to Jeremiah and to us is very clear. God is working constantly to make his creation good once again. We human beings ruin God's good world with our sin and rebellion against his will, attempting to be our own deities and to fashion our own future. The result is strife between male and female, between brother and brother, between nations, with God's creation marred by "thorns and thistles," the God-given gifts of beauty and work turned into ugliness and drudgery, all community becomes impossible, and over it all the sentence of death (Genesis 3-11). Now God works tirelessly to turn our cursed existence into blessing (Genesis 12:3) and to give to all humanity the gift of abundant life, in a community of justice and love and peace that knows how to live for the Lord.

God lays his plans for the salvation of his world very carefully. He tells Jeremiah, "Before I formed you ... before you were born,"

(v. 5). Before the prophet was ever conceived in the womb, God knew his task for Jeremiah, and "consecrated" him, that is, set him apart, to be his prophet. In like manner, God knew and planned each one of us for a special role in his purpose. God does not create human beings simply for nothing. For each of us he has a purpose before he ever makes us.

God equips Jeremiah for his task by putting his words in Jeremiah's mouth (v. 9). In other words, Jeremiah's prophecy is not the result of his own thought. He has not pondered the state of his society or read "the signs of the times," and decided that he simply must speak out against them. Nor has his prophecy been the result of his own religious zeal and indignation or even love for his people — and he does love them dearly. No. Jeremiah's prophetic proclamations are words from the Lord, given to him as gifts from God. His prophecies come from God alone (cf. 15:16), and when Jeremiah tries to say something different, God rebukes him sternly (cf. 15:19). In the same manner, our tasks done for the Lord are made possible by gifts given to us. In the Epistle lesson of 1 Corinthians 13, the faith, hope, and love that Christians are to manifest in their lives are not products of their own thought and work, but gifts of the Spirit, as Paul makes very clear. Apart from God's equipment of us, we cannot do the Lord's work.

The task given to Jeremiah is fearful. He is not only to "build and to plant," not only to comfort and give hope to his people, which he does after the fall of Jerusalem to the Babylonians in 587 B.C. (Jeremiah chs. 30 and 31 are often called "The Book of Comfort"). Jeremiah is also to "pluck up and break down" (1:10), to utter those powerful, active words of judgment that will work their effect in Judah's life until they bring about the nation's downfall. (The concept of the Word of God in the Bible is that it acts in human life to bring about that of which it speaks. Cf. Isaiah 55:10-11; Ezekiel 12:28.)

The reason for the judgment of God in Judah's life, and in ours, is clear. God cannot give us new life without first ridding us of the old. New wine cannot be put into old wineskins, nor the new patch sewn on an old garment (Matthew 9:16-17). We cannot lead Christian lives while preserving our old habits of sin. God uses his judgments on us daily to rid us of our evil ways, in order that he may make us new creatures in Jesus Christ. He will not leave us alone in our evil, because he loves us and does not want us to die the death that our sin deserves. Rather, he constantly works to rid us of evil in order that he may give us a life of good.

It is not surprising that Jeremiah is told he will meet opposition. In fact, 1:18-19 tells us that all in Judah will fight against the prophet, because the Judeans do not, any more than we, like to hear that they are in the wrong. Christians in our day meet opposition, too. It is not easy to be good in our society, in which goodness is out of fashion. Divorce is rampant in our day, as are adultery and abortion, cheating and lying, selfishness and pride. Anyone who lives by God's word these days meets snickers and scorn and sometimes persecution. They are "nerds," "squares," and worst of all, "irrelevant."

But Jeremiah is given the promise of God that is given also to us. "Be not afraid of them," says the Lord, "for I am with you to deliver you" (v. 8). In the midst of every trial that confronts a Christian, who tries to live in faith, hope, and love, God is present with his own to strengthen and guide and reassure that his is the way and truth and abundant life.

Fifth Sunday after Epiphany

Isaiah 6:1-8 (9-13)

We use the word "holy" a lot. We talk about the Holy Bible or the Holy Ghost, a holy place, or a holy person. Roman Catholics call their pope "His Holiness," which is the title of a book about John Paul II. And we sense that when some things or some persons are called "holy," there is a different aura about them. Somehow they seem set apart from our profane, everyday life, and we are tempted to speak in whispers about them.

We are not wrong in the way we treat holiness. The root meaning of the word, "to be holy," is to be set apart, to belong to the realm of the divine. A holy person or a holy place is one set apart for God's purpose. Holiness belongs to God.

So it is that the center of this account by Isaiah of his call to be a prophet in 746 B.C. is that song of the seraphim in verse 3. "Holy, holy, holy is the Lord of hosts." In contrast to the intimate nature of God that we noted in the call of Jeremiah last Sunday, this prophetic call emphasizes God's holiness. That is, it emphasizes God's total otherness from the world of human beings, God's qualitative difference from the things of earth, God's unique divinity that belongs to him alone. The God of the Bible is no soul of nature, no spark within human beings, no familiar spirit available everywhere. No. The God of Old Testament and New is other from everything in heaven and on earth, uniquely different, uniquely holy.

Isaiah says he saw the holy God sitting upon a throne, high and lifted up — a fantastic statement. Isaiah, in the prophetic ecstasy given to the prophets, has entered the heavenly realm in this account, and is granted a vision of God enthroned in the heaven of heavens that is given to few others, according to the Bible (cf. Exodus 24:10; Numbers 12:8).

We in our naive curiosity would immediately ask, "What did God look like?" But the appearance of God is never described in the Bible, just as the appearance of Jesus Christ is never described, for no one can see God and live (cf. Numbers 12:20; Deuteronomy 5:25-26). His glory and majesty are too overwhelming for sinful human beings to stand. So in every vision of God, the attention shifts, and only God's surroundings are described.

Often that description is given in spatial terms. The greatness of God is portrayed by saying he fills everything (cf. Ephesians 1:23). Here in this passage, God's kingly robe fills the heavenly temple; the temple itself is filled with smoke (cf. Revelation 15:8); and God's glory fills the earth (cf. Exodus 40:34-35; Ezekiel 43:5). This God overwhelms everything in his greatness.

As a result, even the seraphim, those winged serpent-like creatures of fire that are God's messengers, cannot bear to look at the Lord. They are six-winged, and with two of those wings they must cover their faces, and with two they must shield their bodies from the light of God's glory. With two, however, they hover in flight, waiting to speed off immediately at the Lord's command.

God's otherness is contrasted with all things earthly in this vision. He is other than any earthly king, even when that human king has been as great as Judah's Uzziah. Uzziah had enlarged Judah's territory, expanded her army, and improved her agriculture. But when Uzziah died of leprosy, Isaiah saw the real King, the Lord of heaven and earth. "The King mine eyes have seen!" he cries out (in the order of the Hebrew words), "the Lord of hosts!"

That King of the universe whom Isaiah sees is also totally other in his moral purity, and over against that absolute righteousness, Isaiah sees his own sinfulness and that of his people. "Woe is me," he exclaims, "for I am lost!" That is, "I am going to die." Measured against the pure righteousness of God, none of us deserves to live. Peter has the same reaction in the Gospel lesson of Luke 5:1-11. "Depart from me," he cries to Jesus, because Peter is sinful, and his sin and the sinless Lord cannot exist together. Is that not always the way we suddenly recognize how far short of the glory of God we have fallen, when we are given a glimpse of the pure goodness of God? And in reaction, do we just try to be rid of God? Or do we fall in repentance at his feet, pleading his mercy?

Surely, the total otherness of God's mercy toward us is evident, too, in what happens to Isaiah. We would condemn a sinner and think he deserves only punishment, excluding ourselves from the judgment, of course. But not this God of total mercy. His seraph messenger cleanses Isaiah's lips with the burning coal of love, and Isaiah is forgiven by his God and prepared for his prophetic mission. The God who is totally other in his kingly glory over all the earth, nevertheless is totally mercy, paying heed to his individual servant.

Only then, in the forgiveness of God, can the prophet hear God's voice, and that too is instructive for us. For when we enter into worship before this Holy God, the King of all life, the Lord of hosts, our first act when we realize God's presence in the midst of our congregation is to confess our sins. And only when God forgives our sins in the Assurance of Pardon can we then hear God speaking to us through the Holy Scripture and sermon. Cleansed, given a new beginning by the love and mercy of God, we can then hear plainly what it is that God desires of us.

Like all the prophets, and indeed, like us, Isaiah is given a task. He is sent to announce God's Word to his people. But the awful Word he has to deliver is one of judgment on Judah's sin. In fact, Isaiah hears that his preaching to Judah will simply make Judeans more stubborn in their rebellion against God, until they deserve even more the judgments that are coming upon them. Isaiah hears from the first that his mission will result in failure! And he cries out in agony, "How long, O Lord?" How long must he preach such a Word?

Would we undertake ministries for God if we were told from the beginning that they would be failures? Faith, it seems, is always up against opposition, and does not seem to make much difference in our world. After all, our Lord Jesus preached and healed and taught for many months, pouring himself out for God's purpose, and the only reward he seemed to get was an agonizing death on a cross. Christians who dedicate themselves to the service of God can often seem to meet the same fate, their work and words seemingly ineffectual in a world like ours full of wrong.

But was God's purpose defeated on the cross of Calvary? Was Christ's work a failure in the on-going activity of God? The Epistle lesson tells us otherwise. Christ was raised from the dead and appeared to hundreds. Our Holy God, our majestic King, our Lord of the hosts of heaven and earth, works in a silent, mysterious way toward the establishment of his kingdom on this earth. That which seems weak is shown to be ultimate strength, and that which is failure wins the victory. And so when we hear God saying to us, "Whom shall I send, and who will go for us?" we can with confidence give Isaiah's reply, "Here am I, Lord. Send me."

Sixth Sunday after Epiphany

Jeremiah 17:5-10

In many respects religious faith has become a rather casual affair in our society. Persons can have it, or they can leave it alone. It's all a matter of personal opinion. There is no particular opprobrium leveled at the person who claims to be an agnostic or atheist, nor is there considered to be much advantage to claiming that one is a Christian. To be sure, at election time, every politician will claim to be deeply religious in order to secure the faithfuls' vote. But otherwise, everyone goes his or her own way, believing or unbelieving, church-goer or Sunday-golfer. It's just a matter of one's own personal choice.

The same is true with respect to discussions about God. He can be a hotly-debated topic, set out to be examined. Is he good or is he indifferent? Can we trust him or is trust misplaced? Is he in control of the world or are we on our own? Does he judge us or doesn't he care? Each person forms her or his own position, and while the questions make for lively group discussion, they really boil down to individual opinion. In the end their answers seem of little consequence in how we live day by day.

In fact, one can be entirely neutral in all religious discussion, taking neither the side of belief nor the side of unbelief, exercising a kindly skepticism toward all positions of faith. And that stance too is considered to be of no particular consequence. "It really does not matter what people believe" said one neighbor to me, "just as long as they are happy." Happiness, contentment, satisfaction, not love of God, are the ultimate goal of living.

At the base of such casual attitudes toward God and Christian faith is another fundamental belief, however, the belief that we have no continuing connection with God. According to the scriptures, you and I and all people have been created in the image of God. That means that we always stand in some sort of relationship with him, and we cannot be fully understood as human beings except that relationship be included. The many areas of human learning may describe us in various terms, from the standpoint of psychology, sociology, economics, history, geography, and so forth. But unless that description includes the fact that we also stand in constant relation to God, we have not been fully described.

As a result, our Old Testament wisdom text for the day — and indeed, all three of our stated texts — say that there are only two ways of life. There is life lived in trust in God, and there is life lived apart from that trust. And between those two alternatives, there is no neutral ground. Paul would put it quite sharply: Either we are slaves of Jesus Christ or we are slaves of sin (cf. Romans 6). There is no neutral ground that we can choose between those two bonds.

What is more, says our text, it makes all the difference in our life as to which position we choose. We have all seen the effects of failing to water a garden. Shrubs and flowers that are green and glorious begin to yellow and droop. The ground around them becomes hard as stone, and in a few weeks the plants dry up and die, leaving only brown twigs in the iron-like earth to mark where they have been. Such is the life of persons who trust only in themselves and other human beings to protect and secure their lives, says Jeremiah. Using the terms of his landscape, he says they are like shrubs in a desolate desert, planted in earth full of salt. There is no growth, no blossoming, no prolongation of their life. Neither in life nor in death do they abide.

In contrast, proclaims our prophet, the one who trusts in the Lord is like a tree planted by a stream of flowing water, and to that water Jeremiah elsewhere compares the Lord (Jeremiah 2:13). Such a person is grounded and rooted in the life of God who never dies. So the person can bring forth good fruit in his or her life, fruit of the Spirit given by God (cf. Galatians 5:22-23). And in the heat of the day, vitality remains, unaffected by circumstance.

Significantly, Jeremiah centers trust in the heart (vv. 5, 10). It is there, in the inmost part of our being, that the prophets locate our dependence on God, for as Jesus says, it is what comes out of a person, out of the heart, that defiles him (Mark 7:14-23). If the heart is sound, life and good action flow out naturally, but if the heart is corrupt, out of it come evil thoughts and deeds. Thus, in his judgment on the Judeans, Jeremiah can say at the beginning of chapter 17 that the sin of Judah is engraved with a point of diamond on the heart (v. 1), and Ezekiel can call for the people to get themselves a new heart lest they die (Ezekiel 18:31). We are called to love God with all our heart (Mark 12:30; Deuteronomy 6:5), as well as with our soul and mind and strength, for it is in our hearts, as we all know, that our love abides. If we love persons with all our heart, we cherish them and try to please them and want to be with them. And so too, and much more, is to be the love and trust in our hearts for God.

Our text tells us that if we dedicate our hearts in love for God, and trust him with our lives in all things, we need not "fear when heat comes" (v. 8). And indeed, if our lives are firmly planted in God, what is there that can harm us? Suffering may come our way — and it comes to all of us — but God is there to comfort and to strengthen. Misfortunes and disappointments may mar our days, but even they can work for good in God's plans for our lives, if we love him (Romans 8:29). Death itself will meet us all, but in God's love, death is not final. Beyond the grave, there is the joyful promise of eternal life with the Father.

God examines our hearts, says our text, verse 10. We cannot escape that. Casual as we sometimes are about our religious faith, indifferent as someone may be to God and the things of God, the One in whose image we were created and with whom we are inextricably connected, sees and knows all that goes on in the depths of our inner selves. God created us in the first place, and now he knows us through and through. And before each one of us he sets that choice of faith, to live in him, nourished by his everlasting life and flourishing in his vitality, or to live for ourselves and meet the inevitable death that comes from our own meager resources. Jesus encapsulated the thought of our text when he set before us those two ways: Whoever saves his own life, relying on self and the world, will lose his life. But whoever loses his life, dedicating it totally to God, will save it (cf. Mark 8:35).

Transfiguration Sunday

Exodus 34:29-35

Perhaps some of you have seen Michelangelo's great marble statue of Moses. Or if you have just seen a picture of that statue, you know that it depicts Moses sitting, holding the tablets of the law. And strangely enough, on Moses' head are two tiny horns. That depiction furnishes us with a good lesson in the history of Old Testament manuscripts. The verb "shone" in verse 29 of our text can also be translated as "horned," and that apparently was the rendering that the Exodus manuscript available to Michelangelo used. It said that Moses' face (or head) was "horned." So that is the way Michelangelo depicted him. Moses had horns.

What our text really says, of course, is that when Moses came down from Mount Sinai after talking with God, the skin of his face "shone." It shone so brilliantly that the people were afraid to draw near to him. But when Moses called them, Aaron and all the leaders and congregation of the people approached Moses and listened to the commands that God had given them through Moses. And whenever Moses gave the people the commandments or whenever he went into the "tent of meeting" (Exodus 33:7-11) to talk with God, Moses left his shining face uncovered. Otherwise, he covered it with a veil, so the shining could not be seen.

All of that is very strange to us, and we need to know what it means. Why did Moses' face shine? It shone with the reflected light of God's glory. We are familiar with the phrase "the glory of God." For example, we read at Christmas that when the angels appeared to the shepherds, "The glory of the Lord shone around them" (Luke 2:9). But what is meant by the glory of the Lord?

God's glory has two meanings throughout the scriptures. First, his glory can designate the esteem and honor in which God is held. The basic meaning of the Hebrew verb, "to be glorious," is "to have weight." And we have the same usage in English. We say that someone has "great weight" in the community. So when we are called upon to give God glory, that means we are called to give him great weight, to deem him esteemed and honored throughout the world.

But the other meaning of God's glory is the meaning found in our text for the morning. God's glory is the shining light effulgence that surrounds his Person. God dwells in "unapproachable light," says the New Testament (1 Timothy 6:16). When he descends to the tabernacle to dwell in the midst of his people, in Exodus 40:34-35, a cloud fills the tabernacle, and in the midst of that cloud is God's shining, glorious light. Thus, Ezekiel 10:4 can speak of the "brightness of the glory of the Lord." God's glory is dazzling light, that gives the dazzling whiteness of Jesus' garments in the story of the Transfiguration and that alters Jesus' countenance.

In our text, therefore, Moses has been speaking with God on Mount Sinai, and when Moses comes down from the mountain, his face shines with the reflected light of God's glory. We know how a person's face can glow with the reflected light of a fire. So too Moses' face glows with the reflected light of God.

It is significant in our text that when Moses is giving the commandments of God to the people, he leaves his face uncovered, and the light of God shines forth. Thus, the text testifies to the fact that the commandments that Moses is giving are in fact the Word of God. Moses' shining face becomes the testimony to the truth that the commandments are God's Word to his people.

Are the commandments of the Old Testament then also God's words to us and therefore to be obeyed, all of those laws and statutes that we find scattered through the Torah, the first five books of our Bibles?

Obviously the Apostle Paul does not think so, according to our Epistle lesson in 2 Corinthians 3:12—4:2. Paul reinterprets our Old Testament text in such a manner that the commandments become the "veil" whereby God is hidden from us, whereas God's revelation of himself in Christ removes the veil and allows us to know the glory of God. "We have seen the light of the knowledge of the glory of God in the face of Christ" (2 Corinthians 4:6). Christ reveals God's true, glorious Person, in a manner impossible for the Mosaic law to do.

72

Before we throw out the Old Testament, however, with its laws and its commandments, we need to take heed of the way in which the New Testament uses those. Our Lord Jesus clearly believes Moses was giving true words of God, because Jesus takes the two central commandments of the Old Testament as the two greatest commandments for us. When one of the scribes asks our Lord, "Which commandment is the first of all?" Jesus quotes to him the words of Deuteronomy 6:4: "Hear, O Israel. The Lord our God, the Lord is one; and you shall love the Lord your God with all your heart, and with all your soul, and with all your mind, and with all your strength." And to that central commandment to love God, Jesus adds the second from Leviticus 19:18: "You shall love your neighbor as yourself." In similar fashion, Jesus affirms the validity of the Ten Commandments for our Christian life, and Mark 10:17-21 tells us that Jesus loves the one who keeps such laws.

The question to ask ourselves when we read — and I hope we often read — the commandments of Moses in the Old Testament is, "Are these commandments reaffirmed for us in the New Testament?" Do Jesus and Paul and the rest of the New Testament figures pick them up and apply them to the Christian life also? Over and over again, such is the case, even in the letters of Paul. After all, our Lord said that he came not to abolish the law and the prophets, but to fulfill them (Matthew 5:17).

Contrary to our Epistle lesson, then, are we to live under the law? Does the Christian faith have about it a legalism after all? As Paul emphasizes, the answer is, "No." What Paul repeatedly underscores is that we are not saved by following the law, that is, we do not enter into relationship with God by obeying commandments. Rather, we are saved solely by grace through our trust in Jesus Christ, who fulfills the law for us. The commandments, then, found in the law and prophets and indeed, throughout the New Testament, are given us as guides in the new life which we have already been given by the death and resurrection of Jesus Christ.

You and I are given a new beginning, a new life by the work of our Lord. "The old has passed away" — the old dispensation in our Epistle lesson: "Behold, the new has come" (2 Corinthians 5:17). And God gives us commandments from Old and New Testament alike to guide our steps in that new life. Mercifully, God goes with us in his commandments, as Israel always believed (cf. Deuteronomy 30:14), showing us how to live with him and our neighbors and all the world in abundant and joyful new life.

Ash Wednesday

Joel 2:1-2, 12-17

Karl Barth once remarked that the greatest tragedy in human life would be to come to the end of our days and to realize that we have been totally worthless in the purpose of God. Or in the thought of our Epistle lesson, at the end to realize that God has poured out his grace on us through all our years, and yet we have done nothing with it (2 Corinthians 6:1).

It is that "end" that the prophet Joel is preaching about in our Old Testament lesson, the end of our lives, and in fact, the end of human history. Joel 2:1-2 concerns the Day of the Lord, the *dies irae* as it is called in so much music and liturgy. That is the final day, when God comes to earth to destroy all of his enemies and to establish his reign over all things and persons. Thus verses 1-2 of our text picture the blowing of the war trumpet, and God's army of heavenly hosts poised to do the final battle against the Lord's foes (cf. 2:11).

Joel has been reminded of that final Day by the devastating locust plague and drought that have devoured Judah's life in the last quarter of the fifth century B.C. (ch. 1). But those were only God's provisional warnings about sin, in the thought of the prophet, and Judah may recover from those. That from which no one can recover, however, and that which no one can escape is God's final judgment on his day of "darkness and gloom" (v. 2). Some Ash Wednesday liturgies of the church remind us of those facts by the ritual of marking our foreheads with ashes, while the minister says the words, "Remember that you are mortal."

"Remember that you are mortal," that is, remember that you are going to die. Death comes to all of us, and the question is, "What then?" We Americans glibly think, of course, that after our deaths, we shall all automatically have eternal life. Of course there is life after death, we believe, and of course we shall all enjoy it.

We like automatic things, you see — automatic coffee, automatic shifts on our automobiles, automatic office doors, automatic happiness in marriage, and so too automatic life after death. Few of us stop to tremble before the specter of death, as our text pictures people trembling (2:1). In our day, some even seek out death with the help of physician-assisted suicide.

But have we stopped to consider the fact that at the end we shall meet God? And that his will be the final judgment as to whether we live or die eternally? Indeed, has the world considered the fact that when God comes to set up his kingdom on earth, his will be the judgment of all the peoples? Jesus pictures that judgment on the Day of the Lord very vividly in the twenty-fifth chapter of Matthew. All nations are assembled before Christ, in that portrayal, and to some he says, "Come ... inherit the kingdom prepared for you" (v. 34), but to others he commands, "Depart from me, you cursed, into the eternal fire ..." (v. 41). And the judgment is made on the basis of whether or not people have served Christ by serving the least among their neighbors, the hungry, the thirsty, the stranger, the naked, and the imprisoned.

We all face a final judgment by God. On this Ash Wednesday, on the basis of our text and innumerable other scripture passages, let's take that as a fact.

But the message to us from the prophet Joel is not all darkness and gloom, for through his prophet, God utters that, "Yet even now." "Yet even now ... return to me ... return to the Lord," we are urged twice in our passage (vv. 12, 13). Even now, in the midst of our sinful ways, when we have been so busy with our own affairs that we have repeatedly neglected others; even now when we have forgotten to rely on God and have counted on our own self-sufficiency; even now when we have burdened our souls with pride and anger and guilt; even now when we think we do not have a prayer with which to stand before the Lord our God — even now, in your situation and mine, God spreads wide his arms of mercy on a cross and bids us return to him.

Surely that cross manifests the description of God that Joel gives us. The Lord is gracious and merciful, slow to anger, and abounding in steadfast love, says our prophet, and he is always willing to turn aside his judgment (v. 13). Joel tells his fellow Judeans that God will even give them the means to make their daily sacrifices in the temple, so they can restore their communion with God (v. 14). But it is through the death and resurrection of Jesus Christ that God offers a return to us. The way is open to the Father. The deed has been done. Christ has cleared the stumbling blocks of our sins that would keep us from walking the path back to God.

Joel even gives directions in how to return to the Father. "Rend your hearts and not your garments," he preaches. His reference to the tearing of garments is to the Israelite practice of repentance, when grief over one's sin was expressed by rending one's garments, by fasting, by covering the head with ashes (thus, Ash Wednesday), by weeping and by prayers like that of the priest in verses 15-17. But those were all external rituals which could be done apart from the engagement of the heart, just as are so many of our Lenten practices of giving up some sort of food or of attending special worship services or of performing special acts. God, the prophet is proclaiming, does not want externals, however. God wants our hearts. God wants sincere, heartfelt repentance which leads to the amendment of our total lives. In fact, that is what repentance means. To "repent" is to "turn around," to go in the opposite direction, to lead a different, God-directed life from the self-directed life we have led before. True repentance is strenuous exercise of the will, taking ourselves in hand, determining every morning to walk in God's way and not in our own. True repentance involves a new heart, a new love for our heavenly Father.

The last part of our text therefore calls for a fast of repentance on the part of all the Judeans (vv. 15-17). No one is excepted, any more than any one of us here this morning is excepted. The whole congregation, including infants and newly-married, are called to the temple, to repent and pray before God, to let their lives be so transformed by the Lord that they practice a new way of life.

Is that an invitation that all of us gathered here in this sanctuary will accept? Will we all replace our little Lenten practices with true amendment of our lives? Will we truly be God's people, loving him with all our hearts, studying his Word, worshiping his name, praying to him daily, and showing mercy and justice to our neighbors? The way is open to that amendment. Christ will give you his Spirit to walk in it. We simply have to open our hearts to him and let him have our committed lives.

First Sunday in Lent

Deuteronomy 26:1-11

Our biblical, Christian faith is basically a response to a story, to the story of what God has done in human history. It is not as if Christians through the ages have looked at the natural world and decided that there must be a God who created it. They have not thought up a picture of God and designed worship to go with the picture. Nor have they adjusted to their changing cultural and social situations simply by drawing up their own rules for the ethics and morals by which we should live. There are some forms of faith in our day that are such products of human imagination and construction. But that is not true of the biblical faith of the Christian Church. No. Our faith is a response to a history of God's words and deeds, a history that is now preserved and passed on to us in the scripture.

So it is that when we confess our faith in the Apostles' Creed, for example, we tell the story on which that faith is based, and the story is the history of what God has done: "I believe in God the Father Almighty, Maker of heaven and earth ... I believe in Jesus Christ, his only Son our Lord, who was born of the virgin Mary, suffered under Pontius Pilate, was crucified, dead, and buried. The third day he rose again from the dead...." On that basis, then, we respond and say, "I believe."

God's acts always come first. We did not construct our faith out of our own thoughts and desires. Rather, God did particular deeds and said particular words, and we say, "Yes, I believe God did those things and spoke those words," and then we work out our response of faith in accord with what the deeds and words have revealed to us about God. Thus, in our Epistle lesson from Romans 10:8b-13, Paul writes that whoever believes and confesses that God raised Jesus from the dead and made him Lord, will be saved. Faith and salvation rest on God's prior act in Jesus Christ.

So it is, too, in our text for the day. This text embodies one of the oldest practices and confessions of faith found in the Old Testament, probably dating back to the twelfth century B.C. It tells of bringing the first fruits of all crops to the sanctuary as an offering to God (cf. Exodus 23:19; 34:26), in recognition of the fact that God is the Owner and Giver of the promised land to Israel. And when the worshiper brings those first fruits, he tells why he is doing so by reciting the confession of faith that is found in verses 5-9.

What that confession of faith is, however, is the basic story of God's acts that are recorded for us in the Hexateuch, made up of the books of Genesis through Joshua. The confession tells of the patriarch, Jacob, going down into Egypt; of the multiplication of the Israelites, in accord with God's promise to Abraham; of their enslavement by the Egyptians; of God's delivery of them out of slavery "with a mighty hand and an outstretched arm, with great terror, with signs and wonders" (v. 8); and of the gift of the land to them in the time of Joshua, again in fulfillment of the promise to Abraham. The worshiper is bringing the gift of the first fruits, because God has done all of those things, in fulfillment of his promise. The worshiper's act is a response to God's act. He believes the sacred story, and he responds in confession and practice.

The notable thing in this confession, further, is that all of those acts of God in Israel's life are not considered by the worshiper to be acts done just in the distant past for his forbears. Rather, they are acts done also for him. "The Egyptians treated *us* harshly," he says, "and afflicted *us*." "*We* cried to the Lord." "The Lord heard *our* voice," "saw *our* affliction," "brought *us* out of Egypt," "gave *us* this land." God's acts of salvation were done not just in the past, but also for each new generation of Israelites, who reap the benefits of those acts in the present.

We have a sacred story of God's acts of salvation in the past too, don't we? And it is very much like Israel's story. We too were slaves once — slaves to sin and death — but God sent us a Deliverer to redeem us out of our slavery and to give us a new life in the "glorious liberty of the children of God." As with Israel at Mount Sinai, God entered into covenant with us also by means of that Deliverer, and he gave us his commandment to love one another as

80

he has loved us. Like Israel trekking through the wilderness, we too set out on a journey toward a promised land that still lies before us. And like Israel we are accompanied every step of the way by the One who said that he is with us always.

None of that is simply history in the past, however, any more than Israel's story was just in the past. No. Those are all things that God has done and is doing for each of us this day. This day, by the cross and resurrection of Jesus Christ, we are delivered from sin and death. This Sunday or on the Sunday when we sit at the Lord's table, we enter anew into covenant with him and are given his commandments of love. This day, you and I are journeying toward a promised land that is known as the Kingdom of God. And this day, Christ is with us on the journey, and promises to be with us always. All of that sacred story from the Bible is our story. And if we believe that story with all our hearts and confess it with our lives and act accordingly, we too shall be saved.

Two further things should be said. The worshiper in our Deuteronomy text knows the story. He knows his people's history of what God has done in their lives, and the result is that he can tell the story, not only there at the sanctuary, but also to his children and grandchildren. Can we do the same? Do we know the biblical history, that is given us in the scriptures, so well that we can tell it to others and to our offspring? Do we know the accounts of God's deeds and words in New Testament and Old? Or are they rather hazy memories from past years in Sunday school or occasional Bible classes? Our faith is a response to God's acts and words, preserved for us in the scriptures, but if we do not know the scriptures, we have no solid basis for our faith. In this Lenten season, perhaps the one thing we should all do is read the Bible every day.

Second, our text tells us that the Israelite worshiper, when he brings his offering, can rejoice "in all the good which the Lord your God has given to you." His worship can be joyful, because he knows the wonderful deeds that God has wrought on his behalf. And the same is true for us. If we know what God has done for us, if we know the benefits of his deeds and words, there is simply no other response we can make in the worship of this church than to rejoice. In the words of our text, we can rejoice because God has

81

heard our voice, and seen our affliction, our toil, and our oppression. We can rejoice because he has delivered — and delivers us daily — from our slavery to the sin of this world and from the terrible defeat that death would mean. We can rejoice because our Lord is with us here, accompanying us on our journey. And we can rejoice because there lies before us his kingdom of good and love and eternal life.

Second Sunday in Lent

Genesis 15:1-12, 17-18

The preacher who confronts the three stated texts for this Sunday once again faces the confusing situation of wondering how on earth the three lessons are related. Perhaps several answers are possible, but to my mind, all three of them have to do with living by a promise.

In the context of our Genesis text, Abraham and Sarah and their households have obeyed the command of God and left Ur of the Chaldees (v. 7; cf. 11:31), settled temporarily at Haran in Mesopotamia, and then journeyed on to Canaan, the land that God showed them. They were promised that the land would belong to them and their descendants, and that they would become the forbears of a great nation (Genesis 12:1-7).

Now, however, Abraham and his company simply wander through the land that still belongs to the Canaanites. Both Abraham and his wife Sarah are old, past the age of childbearing, and the promises that the Lord gave them in the past seem impossible of fulfillment. The future that God previously laid out before them was apparently nothing but a dream and an empty assurance that had caused them to leave everything familiar and to become pilgrims and wanderers in a foreign country. It is in that situation, without hope for the future, that our text begins.

A mysterious and hidden God appears to Abraham in this passage. His Word comes to the aged man, first in a vision (v. 1), and then in a dream (v. 12), and his presence is indicated by the strange symbols at night of a smoking fire pot and flaming torch (v. 17). Nevertheless, his words are spoken to Abraham.

The first Word is that Abraham will have many posterity: "Your reward will be very great" (v. 1), and Abraham simply does not believe that Word. In fact, in response to the promise that he will have many descendants, Abraham blasphemously replies in so many words, "No, I won't. I have no son of my own, and the only heir to be found in my house is the son of my slave-woman, who will inherit all my property, as is the custom in these parts" (vv. 2-3). This father of our faith was no model of unshakable trust in the Lord.

God has a way of never giving up on the recipients of his promises, however, so he takes Abraham outside to look at the stars and to count them, if Abraham is able. And at that point, the Lord renews his promise: "That's how many descendants you will have." More, the Lord inspires in Abraham faith in the promise. "Abraham believed the Lord," reads our text, "and the Lord reckoned it to him as righteousness" (v. 6).

This is the first account of righteousness by faith that we find in the scriptures. The Christian Church has always confessed that we are counted righteous or justified in God's sight by grace through faith alone. Here, our father Abraham becomes the pioneer in that faith.

We should note carefully, however, what faith consists in, for this story also characterizes the faith we are to have. Abraham's faith in the Lord consists in the fact that he believes God's promise, despite all appearances to the contrary, and so Abraham will act from now on as if that promise will come true. God has now opened the future to him and assured him that he will have a son, from whom will spring those many descendants that the Lord has said he will have. Abraham has simply to wait for the promise to be fulfilled.

The same is true in the remainder of the stated lesson. In the mysterious and awesome dream of sacrifice that Abraham undergoes, God promises that he will also give to Abraham's descendants the land on which Abraham is sleeping, from the border of the Nile to the Euphrates in the North. (The borders are those of the davidic empire.) More than that, in the strange symbolism of passing through the cut pieces of the sacrifice, God himself promises that he will be destroyed, like the cut animals, if he does not keep his Word! Once again, Abraham is called upon simply to wait for the promise's fulfillment, despite all the evidence against it.

Our life with God is very much like father Abraham's, for we too have been given lots of promises by our Lord. "Lo, I am with you always, to the close of the age" (Matthew 28:20). "Whoever would save his life will lose it; and whoever loses his life for my sake and the gospel's will save it" (Mark 8:35). "Fear not, little flock, for it is your Father's good pleasure to give you the kingdom" (Luke 12:32). "I will not leave you desolate; I will come to you" (John 14:18). "He who believes in me, though he die, yet shall he live, and whoever lives and believes in me shall never die" (John 11:25-26).

Faith, therefore, consists in believing those promises and acting as if they will come true. To be sure, the evidence seems often against the fulfillment of Christ's words. When we are beset by trouble on every side, or when pain is our daily fare; when every circumstance seems to go against us and there seems to be no hope for the future; when we sacrifice for the sake of the gospel and find no peace or reward whatsoever; when we stand beside the grave of a loved one, and sorrow washes over us, do Christ's promises of his presence, of his peace and joy and abundant life, of his eternal life in the kingdom, do away with the empty desolation and give us a future full of hope? Often all the evidence seems to point in the opposite direction, and we are like those of whom Paul speaks in our Epistle lesson (Philippians 3:17—4:1), with our minds dominated only by the terrible nature of earthly things.

Surely that could have been true also of our Lord as he journeyed toward that cross in Jerusalem. Some kindly Pharisees advised him to flee from his task and to save his own life, according to our Gospel lesson (Luke 13:31-35). What future was there for anyone who died a torturous death? But our Lord's reply was steadfast in his faith that God owned his future. "I finish my course," he replied. "I must go on my way today and tomorrow and the day following; for it cannot be that a prophet should perish away from Jerusalem."

Faith trusts God's promises, despite all the evidence to the contrary. Faith simply waits for God to fulfill those promises, and knows that he will do so. So faith acts in that sure knowledge that the

Word of God will come to pass. And it goes on its way today and tomorrow and the day following, and it finishes its course.

We have lots of evidence to show that it is true. God kept his promises of descendants and land to Abraham. And God kept his promise to our Lord that on the third day he would rise from the dead. So faith is holding fast to the promises of God, no matter what else happens, for God always keeps his Word. We can count on it.

Third Sunday in Lent

Isaiah 55:1-9

On this third Sunday in Lent, all three of our lessons have to do with repentance, but we will look at that specifically in our Isaiah text.

Verses 8 and 9 of our Old Testament lesson tell us about the absolute otherness of God. "My thoughts are not your thoughts, neither are my ways your ways, says the Lord." That is a revelation that we need to remember whenever we try to identify the Lord with theological theories from our own imagination, or whenever we try to say that one of our social programs is identical with the will of God. All of our theologies and philosophies, all of our programs and projects, both in and outside of the church, are tainted by our sinfulness. There is no thought or action of ours for which we can claim absolute truth and authority. Those lie in God alone, whose ways and thoughts are always higher and purer than ours. Thus, we always need the revelation of God's thoughts and ways that are illumined for us by the Holy Spirit and spoken to us through the scriptures. Apart from that biblical revelation, we do not know God's ways and will for us.

The specific character of God that is emphasized in verses 8 and 9 of our passage, however, is his incredible, forgiving mercy. We human beings do not forgive very readily. If someone has ignored us for most of our life, we have eliminated her from our list of friends and treated her with indifference. If certain persons have said all sorts of evil things about us, we have counted them as our enemies and often vowed revenge. If others have accused us of wrong against them, we have treated them with scorn or ridicule.

But not God. Those have never been God's reactions. Israel, languishing in Babylonian exile after 587 B.C., was in that country of captivity because she had ignored her God and run after false gods and blasphemed God's holy name. And now, what does God say to her through his prophet Second Isaiah? "Return to me, for I will have mercy on you and will abundantly pardon." It reminds us of the words of our Lord on the cross when the nails held him up against the sky, "Father, forgive them, for they know not what they do" (Luke 23:34). Despite all the indifference and wrong with which we have treated our Lord, he holds out to us the invitation to return and to be forgiven. And surely, God is totally other than we in that incredible mercy.

There are lots of further notes that enter into that gracious invitation, according to our scripture lesson. First, the prophet tells us, "Seek the Lord while he may be found, call upon him while he is near" (v. 6). We can't just return to fellowship with our God any old time we feel like it. We can't just willfully break a commandment and then decide, "Okay, I'll find God now." We can't just glibly wrong a neighbor and comfort ourselves with the thought that nevertheless God will forgive and accept us back. No. The initiative lies always with God, and unless he draws near to us and says, "Return," we cannot go back to him.

At a specific time in the sixth century B.C., God drew near to the exiled Israelites, through the word of his prophet, and offered them his forgiveness. And at specific times, God in Christ draws near to us and offers us his mercy. The church has always called those times "the means of grace." And they come to us when the scripture is read or spoken in this church, revealing God's mercy; when the sermon is preached, inviting our return; and when the Supper is celebrated, offering us the forgiveness of Christ on the cross. At those times, through Word, written and spoken, and through sacrament, symbolized by water and bread and cup, God draws near to us and invites us back to himself.

Second, what God says to us at those times, however, is, "Let the wicked forsake his ways, and the unrighteous persons their thoughts" (v. 7). In short, God says to us in his invitation of forgiveness, "Repent. Change your ways. Turn around. Direct your life in the opposite direction toward good. Vow to become a new person in Jesus Christ." No person can truthfully accept the forgiveness of Almighty God, unless that acceptance is accompanied by a sincere desire to walk in newness of life, according to God's

Word of commandment. Do you remember the classic introduction that used to be given to the Lord's Supper?

> *Ye who do truly repent and earnestly repent of your sins ... and intend to lead a new life, following the commandments of God, and walking from henceforth in his holy ways: Draw near with faith and take this Holy Sacrament....* Book of Common Worship

True and earnest repentance, the intention to lead a new life and to follow the commandments of God — in that attitude alone can we accept God's offer of forgiveness and mercy.

Third, the content of the mercy that God holds out to us in his forgiveness is wondrous indeed. Listen to what God offers us in our scripture passage. "Everyone who thirsts, come to the waters; and he who has no money, come buy and eat! Come, buy wine and milk without money and without price" (v. 1). God offers us the water that will quench every thirst for meaning and peace that we have ever had. And he offers us the bread that will satisfy every hunger for God and his good. Do you remember when Jesus said it? "I am the bread of life; those who come to me shall not hunger, and those who believe in me shall never thirst" (John 6:35).

We need that bread of life and that living water, don't we? As our scripture lesson says, we have for many days spent our money for that which does not feed our hunger for goodness and our labor for that which does not satisfy our longings. Buying and selling, laboring and longing, the world's rewards have not fed our souls, and there remains within us a restless desire — for what? Surely for God who created us to live in fellowship with him always.

God offers us that loving fellowship, that deep sense that we are finally home, returned to the family of God, where there are joy and laughter, and honor and goodness, and the peace that the world cannot give. God offers us nothing less than life abundant in his company. "Incline your ear, and come to me," he says in our text, "hear, that your soul may live" (v. 3). And more than that, he tells us he will never abandon us. "I will make with you an everlasting covenant," he promises. Death itself will not separate us from him.

So, everyone who thirsts, come to the waters, and you who hunger, come and eat! God has drawn near to us in Jesus Christ. The way is now open to return home.

Fourth Sunday in Lent

Joshua 5:9-12

Christians live under new conditions. Paul tell us in the Epistle lesson for this Sunday that the old life has been done away and that the new life has begun. We are new creations of God. There are all sorts of metaphors that the Bible uses to describe that Christian passage from old to new. It says that we have been born anew, or that we have passed from slavery into freedom. It proclaims that we have emerged from darkness into light, or from despair into meaning, from mourning into joy, or from death into life. We walk no more by the flesh, but by the Spirit, or we are no longer conformed to the world, but to the will of God. Throughout the scriptures, the newness of life that we have been given in Jesus Christ is emphasized.

Perhaps nowhere is that newness emphasized more than in Paul's description of our baptisms in Romans 6. The apostle tells us that when we were baptized, we died and were buried with Christ. Our old lives, lived solely for ourselves, with all of their sin and guilt, their lack of hope and of a future, their bondage to the world and its evil, were buried six feet under by Christ's death on the cross and his burial. But by the resurrection of Christ, we were raised from the water of baptism to a new life, a new future, a new goodness.

In a moving article in the October 21, 1992, issue of *The Christian Century*, Ralph C. Wood told of the baptism of a man imprisoned for the terrible crime of molesting his ten-year-old daughter. The man's wife and daughter forgave him for his sin, whereby "the molester got on his knees and begged for the mercy of God and his family" (p. 926). As a result, the prison chaplain agreed to baptize him into the Christian faith. The only baptismal "font" available was a plastic-lined wooden coffin, and so the prisoner, burdened with his sin, was lowered by the chaplain into the death of Christ and raised from the waters, washed clean of his past and given a future by the resurrection of Christ. From that time on, he was a new man; after serving his time, he became a faithful father and husband and member of his local church. Thus does the work of Jesus Christ make us new creations.

I tell all of these things from the standpoint of the New Testament, because they serve as a parallel to our Old Testament lesson. The Old Testament parallel to baptism in the New Testament is circumcision. Both baptism and circumcision signal an entrance into the covenant relation with God, and immediately preceding our text, we read that all of the Israelite men who crossed the Jordan with their families and with Joshua into the promised land underwent that covenant rite. They and their families entered into a new life by becoming the covenant people of God. Moreover, to celebrate that new relationship, they celebrated the first passover in the promised land. And to emphasize the newness of their situation even more, we are told in our text that they no longer needed to be fed by God with the manna that had been their food in the wilderness. Rather, now they could eat the produce of the promised land. Everything was fresh and different. The Israelites had begun a new life.

Apparently, the enigmatic sentence in verse 9 of our text is intended also to emphasize that newness, but none of us knows exactly what the verse means by "the reproach of Egypt." Perhaps it refers to the Israelites' previous slavery. Perhaps it is a reference to their previous ignorance of God. Certainly it furnishes a etymological meaning for "Gilgal," the place of Israel's encampment, because the Hebrew verb "to roll," *galal*, sounds very much like the name "Gilgal."

Whatever the precise meaning, the new situation of Israel's life is being emphasized. Now she has a taste of "the glorious liberty of the children of God." God has kept his promises to her forebears. The life of slavery, with its hopelessness and bondage, is in the past. The long forty-year trek through the wilderness, with its thirst and hunger, its deadly serpents and dangers, is behind them. The seemingly difficult passage through the Jordan has been accomplished with the help of God's miracle. Israel, the wandering

92

people, now has a home, commandments to guide her in her new life, and a relationship with the God who will be her refuge and strength through all the future. Israel and we have been given a new beginning. "The old has passed away. Behold, the new has come."

In the thought of the Old Testament, however, Israel also has a mission. She has not been redeemed from slavery and guided through the terrors of the wilderness and given the land simply because God loves her, although that certainly also is the case, as the Old Testament tells us — God always acts in love (cf. Deuteronomy 7:6-8). But God does not redeem his people and enter into covenant with them for no reason. Rather, God chooses and loves his covenant people, because he loves all peoples and has a purpose for all the families of the earth.

We read of that love and purpose at the very beginning of Israel's story in Genesis 12:1-3. Abraham is told at that time that he and his descendants are to be the instruments through which God will bring his blessing on all people. We have corrupted the good world that God made at the beginning, and now God wants to restore the goodness to the world that it has lost. We live under the curse of sin and death, but through Israel, God wants to do away with evil and bring his blessing on all folk.

Israel's new life of settlement in the land of Canaan, therefore, is understood in the Old Testament as her time of testing (cf. Joshua 23:14-16; Judges 3:1-6). Will she be a faithful people, following the will of her Lord, praising his name and serving him in everything she does, so that the other nations will see God's work in her and turn in commitment to the Lord also? If so, then Israel will fulfill her God-given task of being the medium of blessing for all the families of the earth, bringing all nations to worship the one true God. Or will Israel turn to other gods and goddesses and go her own willful way, deserting the task for which God has made her his own?

That is the same task to which you and I and all Christians are called. We too have been redeemed out of slavery to sin and death and given a new beginning, in the glorious liberty of the children of God. But God has chosen us also, and made us his own because we have a mission. We have the calling from God to live such faithful lives, walking according to God's commandments, that other people will see God's work in us too, and be drawn to confess his lordship. We have a new life in Jesus Christ, and we have been given the Spirit of our Lord to enable us to walk and serve in his ways. And now the question for us is, as it was for Israel, will we be faithful? Will we so obey and trust our Lord that he can use us in his purpose of blessing and restoring his world to goodness?

We can have no more meaningful task given us in this life, nor can Jesus Christ equip us more fully for the task than he has already done by his cross and resurrection, by his scripture and his Spirit with us. We have only to accept his call and today begin the mission.

Fifth Sunday in Lent

Isaiah 43:16-21

Endings can be sad. Your son calls you unexpectedly from college and wants nothing more than to tell you about his studies and his new girlfriend, and you're sad when the call has to end. Or you attend the symphony and are swept up by the glorious music and are very sorry when the finale comes. But of course, those are temporary endings.

Other endings are much more permanent. I just retired from seminary teaching after forty years of classroom work. While the newfound freedom and release from duty are pleasant, I am a little sad not to be able any more to watch students grow in their faith and learning, in all of their eagerness and questioning. I'm sure you must have similar sad feelings when you retire too and no longer have the challenge and satisfaction of accomplishment and the daily association with your colleagues.

But saddest of all are those times when a loved relationship comes to an end. One July I visited a friend who was slowly dying of kidney disease from diabetes. She looked healthy enough, but as I prepared to leave, she told me, "I won't see you again, and I want you to know that I love you very much." She died that September. Endings can be very sad indeed.

Of course endings can also some times be joyful. We have a friend in Africa who told us, "Where there's death, there's hope" — hope for release from an oppressive government, hope for a remedy from poverty and tyranny. The endings of injustice, suffering, oppression, prejudice are devoutly to be desired.

Israel, in our Isaiah text, had no such joyful feelings about endings, however. Her life as a nation was at an end. The troops of the Babylonians had swept through her land, burned her temple and houses, broken down the walls of Jerusalem, and carried all but her poorest peasants into exile in Babylonia. Gone were her land, her davidic king, her priests, her temple, her ark of the covenant. She had become "no people," as Psalm 44 says, a "laughingstock" among the nations, an object of taunts and of derision and scorn (vv. 13-14).

What made it worse, according to Psalm 44, was that Israel had a memory. She remembered the days when God had given her victories, when he had pushed down her enemies and saved her from her foes. The previous generations had told her all about those glory days. But now the glory was gone and the Israelites lamented:

> *Yet thou hast cast us off and abased us,*
> *and hast not gone out with our armies ...*
> *Thou has made us like sheep for the slaughter,*
> *and hast scattered us among the nations.*
> *Thou hast sold thy people for a trifle,*
> *demanding no high price for them.*
>
> Psalm 44:9-10, 12

Israel's life as a people was at an end, because God had deserted her, she was sure. "My way is hid from the Lord," she mourned, "and my right is disregarded by my God" (Isaiah 40:27). The end of a loving human relationship is bad enough, but the end of our relationship with God is worst of all.

The glad news of our text for the morning is that, for God, there are no sorrowful endings. Rather, there is always a future. "Remember not the former things," God tells the exiled Israelites (v. 18). Never mind the glory days of the past. And take no heed of your past sins that led you to your present sorry situation. "Behold, I am doing a new thing; now it springs forth, do you not perceive it?" (v. 19). God has a future for his exiled folk beyond their wildest imagination. According to our text, he will lead them once more out of slavery in a new exodus event. Waters will flow forth in the desert and even the wild beasts will praise his act (vv. 19-20). God will return to his people and lead them into a new life, defending them by his mighty right arm, but also feeding them like a shepherd, carrying them tenderly in his everlasting love, and gently leading those who are with young (40:9-11). The central message of the Second Isaiah, then, is that Israel is to wait for that new act, wait patiently for the God who will save her and renew her life once again (40:28-31).

We should note what kind of God can make such a promise, however. In verses 15-17 of our text, he is the Lord, the Holy One unlike any other, the Creator of Israel, her King. And as that Holy Lord and King, God is the one who defeated the mighty Egyptian Empire and delivered Israel out of Egyptian slavery in the first place. God is the one who has the power to defeat the might of nations, but God is also the one who has the love that can redeem and save his own. And that God, that God alone, is the one who can always give us a future.

God does not deal in permanent endings. And so you are at the end of a loving relationship, but God still has a future for you. You have reached the age of retirement, but God still has you in his plans. You are in a situation where you think you cannot go on, but God can strengthen and guide you on. You are at the end of your rope, but God holds you by a cord of love.

Indeed, some loved one of yours has died and you have been left behind, with nothing but emptiness to fill your days and the feeling that life is over. Christians, however, are those who never have to say goodbye. Beyond the grave, beyond the emptiness, beyond the sorrowful goodbye, there is God's eternal life, and God's joyful reunion of all those who love him, and yes, still the strength and the comfort that can give peace in the midst of loneliness. The resurrection of our Lord Jesus Christ put an end to permanent endings. For the God who redeemed Israel out of slavery had the power and the love to overcome even death.

God has a future for us all, no matter what our situation. "Behold, I am doing a new thing," he tells us. Wait for it and expect it, trusting that he will never forget or forsake you.

Passion/Psalm Sunday

Isaiah 50:4-9a

This is the stated text also in Cycles A and B. The preacher may want to consult those expositions, along with this one.

This is a poem in the writings of Second Isaiah that scholars have long called a "Servant Song," one of the four that occur in this prophetic book. (The others are found in Isaiah 42:1-4; 49:1-6, and 52:13—53:12.) Although the question has been hotly debated for many years, many scholars have said, and I would agree, that the speaker in the Servant Songs is Israel, but it is Israel as she is meant to be, Israel as she is called to be, Israel as God will make her. In short, the one who speaks to us here in our lesson is an ideal Israel of the future. She is called to be the Lord's special servant, who will give her life for the sake of all nations, and who, through her suffering, will draw all nations to the Lord.

Thus, in our passage, Israel hears the Word of the Lord and does not rebel against it, but rather undergoes suffering and scorn for the sake of obeying that Word, in the sure trust that in the end her course will be vindicated by God. So we could read the passage from that standpoint.

Surely, however, the text also says something about the life of the prophet, Second Isaiah, himself. And it is a revealing glimpse into the source of revelation to the prophet. Why does the prophet speak particular words? The answer is that he does not dredge up those words from his own thoughts and imagination. Rather the words are given him by the Lord.

But how does the prophet receive those words? It has always been a mystery to us moderns as to what a prophet means when he says, "Thus says the Lord," or "The Lord of hosts has revealed himself in my ears" (Isaiah 22:14). We have a hard time identifying that with anything in our experience. But Second Isaiah tells us here in our text that God gives him words in the most intimate communion. Every morning the prophet listens, like a pupil listening to a teacher. He opens his ears in prayer, expectant, ready to hear what God says to him, and God speaks. Moreover, the prophet receives those words and obeys them and proclaims them.

Prophets, however, are never very readily received. We human beings don't like our lives interrupted by God. As a result, most of the prophets of the Old Testament are the victims of suffering and scorn. Sometimes kings or queens put prophets to death for defying them (cf. 1 Kings 18:4). Sometimes the populace or religious establishment plots to kill them or puts them in prison or in the stocks (cf. Jeremiah 11:18-19; 20:1-2; 32:1-3). As Jesus mourned when he approached Jerusalem, "O Jerusalem, Jerusalem, killing the prophets and stoning those who are sent to you! How often would I have gathered your children together as a hen gathers her brood under her wings, and you would not" (Luke 13:34). Apparently, therefore, judging from verse 6 of our text, Second Isaiah also suffered for his faithfulness in his ministry. Yet he was sure that God would help him endure the suffering and calumny and that in the end, he would be vindicated and proven right. And the fact that we now have his words in our Bible shows that his faith was not in vain. Sometimes prophets had to wait a long time for their words to be proven true.

When we average Christians approach this lectionary passage, however, most often we interpret it as the words of Jesus Christ. It was not written by the Second Isaiah with Christ in mind; the incarnation had not yet taken place. But surely the New Testament is correct when it says that our Lord fulfills the picture that we have in these songs of the true Servant of the Lord.

Can any one of us doubt that Jesus lived in the most intimate communion with his Father? "The words that I say to you I do not speak on my own authority," he told his disciples; "but the Father who dwells in me does his works" (John 14:10). And so the teachings and commandments that emerge from the mouth of Jesus are the words of God himself.

Further, Jesus is not rebellious, as our text says of the Servant (v. 5). He is tempted in all things as we are, we are told, but he does not sin (Hebrews 4:15). That is, he never loses his trust in his Father in order to follow his own will. His agonized prayer in Gethsemane is, "Father, if thou art willing, remove this cup from me; nevertheless not my will, but thine, be done" (Luke 22:42).

So the awful picture of suffering portrayed in our text (v. 6) is played out in the passion of our Lord. His is the back that is scourged with the whips of Pilate's soldiers. His is the face that is spit upon. His is the beard that is pulled in scorn, until finally the shouts of "Crucify him!" hang him on the cross.

We are told that when Jesus determined to go to Jerusalem to meet his death, he set his face like a stone (Luke 9:51 in the Greek), like the flint in our text (v. 7), in unwavering determination to carry out the will of his Father. For he knew, as the Servant knows in our text, that God would vindicate him and show him righteous in the resurrection on Easter morn. That knowledge did not lessen his suffering, or the torture of the death that awaited him. But it enabled him to undergo crucifixion in the certainty that God would help him (v. 9 in our text).

Suppose, however, that we also read this text for the morning as our words. Because it so accurately pictures the life of our Lord, it is also a model for our Christian living, and it holds up before us the way we are to walk day by day.

First, there is that intimate communion in prayer to God that begins every morning, and that is the undergirding of all Christian living. The words of God now speak to us through the Holy Scriptures, and to know God and to abide in a living fellowship with him is to read those words of scripture expectantly, with eyes and ears open, to hear what God says to us through the Bible. On the basis of that hearing, then, we are to pray, to pray to the Lord whom we know through the scriptures, daily, consistently, eager for his Word. The Christian life cannot be lived nor can it be sustained, except we enter into that daily, intimate communion with our Lord.

Second, there is in our text the determination to be faithful to the Lord, even if it means we will suffer. And we should not delude ourselves about that. If we want to be a faithful Christian in our society we will have to undergo suffering. It is not easy in our society to hold a marriage together in faithfulness, when around us one out of two marriages is failing. It is not easy to believe that the accumulation of wealth and goods is not the goal of living, when advertisers bombard us daily and the whole point of our labor seems to be to show a big profit on the bottom line. It is not easy to practice forgiveness or mercy or love toward others when most people are just out for themselves. It is not easy to believe that God is the Ruler yet, when evil and violence are all around us. Others who watch our activities and hear our beliefs may call us whimps or nerds or squares, or even worst of all, irrelevant and divorced from the "real world." Can we live a good life in a society where goodness is out of fashion, and believe with all our hearts that God's goodness will triumph? Our text for the morning sets forth that sure belief.

Jesus' command to all us disciples was, "Take up your cross and follow me," and if we wish to obey that command, we may expect the words of our Isaiah text to become true in our lives also, as they became true in his. But that means life abundant with God, good Christians, and the glories of Easter morn.

Maundy/Holy Thursday

Exodus 12:1-4 (5-10) 11-14

The same Old Testament text is used for Maundy Thursday in all three cycles of the lectionary. The preacher may therefore wish to consult the expositions in Cycles A and B along with this one.

In the oldest tradition that we have of the celebration of the Lord's Supper, Paul tells us in our Epistle lesson that on the night he was betrayed, Jesus celebrated the Passover with his disciples. While Passover and the Lord's Supper are very different in many respects, they share some features in common. Perhaps those common characteristics can deepen our understanding of what we are about on Maundy Thursday.

As it now stands, the institution of Passover is embedded in the story of the exodus, falling immediately before the account of the final plague on the Egyptians in the form of the death of the firstborn. And it is the Passover ritual that is designed to protect the enslaved Israelites from that plague.

According to the dating in our passage, the Passover is to be celebrated on the fourteenth day of the month of Nisan, which is our March/April. It is a family festival, sometimes shared with a neighbor. The food that is eaten is the food of travelers in a hurry: the unblemished lamb of a sheep or goat, roasted on an open fire, instead of in a cooking pot; bread without leaven, because leavened bread takes too long to rise; bitter herbs that are some kind of uncultivated vegetable, pulled up from the ground. Moreover, the participants are to be prepared for flight, with their long robes pulled up and girded, their sandals on their feet, and their staffs in their hands.

The whole lamb is to be eaten and any parts remaining are to be burned. But the blood of the lamb is to be smeared on the framework of the Israelites' doors. When God sees the blood, he will "pass over" the houses of the Israelites and not slay their children.

The slaying of the firstborn of the Egyptians, however, will prompt the Pharaoh to let Israel go from slavery. Thus, the blood itself is not what saves. Rather, it is a "sign" to God and the symbol of his promise that he will save his people from bondage.

In short, Passover is a celebration of God's redemption of Israel from Egyptian slavery. Moreover, it is at the time of the Passover and exodus that Israel is constituted as a nation and is chosen by God as his people and as his adopted son (cf. Hosea 11:1; Jeremiah 3:19; 31:20; Isaiah 63:16). In every succeeding generation, therefore, Israel is to celebrate the Passover as the memorial of God's redemption of his people.

We share the same memorial, don't we? Our Epistle lesson from 1 Corinthians 11:23-26 tells us that as often as we eat the bread and drink the cup, we "show forth" the Lord's death until he comes again. We remember Jesus' death on the cross. In fact, in the Gospel according to John, Jesus' crucifixion takes place on Passover day. So John the Baptist can call our Lord "the Lamb of God, who takes away the sin of the world" (John 1:29). Similarly, Paul reminds us that "Christ, our paschal lamb, has been sacrificed" (1 Corinthians 5:7). We were "bought with a price," he tells the Corinthians (1 Corinthians 6:20; 7:23). That is, we were "bought back," we were "redeemed," which is the meaning of "redemption," by the death of Christ on the cross. Christ's cross is the New Testament parallel to the story of the Passover and exodus in the Old Testament. As Israel was redeemed from slavery in Egypt, so we are redeemed by the sacrifice of our Lord on Golgotha. And Christ's blood, symbolized for us in the cup of the Lord's Supper, is the "sign" of God's promised redemption, as the blood on the doorposts of the Israelites was the sign of God's promised deliverance of them.

Israel remembers the Lord's redemption of her every time she holds her Passover feast, and we remember Christ's redemption of us every time we celebrate the Lord's Supper. But "remembering" for Israel was much more than simply calling to mind a past event. Rather, when each subsequent generation of Israelites remembered their deliverance from slavery by celebrating the Passover, that became a present event for them. "The Lord brought *us* out of Egypt with a mighty hand," they confessed (Deuteronomy 26:8). We were there. God did his mighty deed for us who are living now. So we are now a free people, chosen by God to be his.

So it is too with us. God's redemption of us by the cross of Christ was not just a past event. It is the redemption of you and me, right now, in our situation. The old Negro spiritual has it right. "Were you there when they crucified my Lord?" it asks. Yes indeed, we were there. Christ died for us. Christ set us free from slavery, our slavery to sin and death. His mighty act of love is wrought for us here and now. And we not only "remember the Lord's death until he comes," but we participate now in the results of that death. We are redeemed and free, redeemed from all of the sins and guilts of the past that held us captive, and free from the clutches of death forever. Right now, at this Lord's table, you and I, are a delivered people.

We all join together in that common deliverance, don't we? As Israel was first made a people at the Passover and exodus, so we too here at the Lord's Supper are united once again as one people of God. This is "communion" at this supper. We are chosen here to commune once again with our God, and to commune once again with one another. And the unity that we share at this supper is not to be broken.

The Israelites were a traveling people, waiting at that first Passover event with their loins girded and their feet shod to set out on the adventure of God. The Lord had a destination for his people and a journey to be undertaken. They were not at home in Egypt. There was a promised land awaiting them. And you and I are not at home where we live either. The land that we inhabit is much too filled with violence and corruption, with evil and hatred to be called God's kingdom. We cannot be satisfied with the status quo, for it does not at all match what God desires for us and for all people. And so God says to us, as he said to Israel, be prepared to travel. Set out on the journey of faith to make your home, your neighborhood, your society into new places worthy of God. Follow the leading of the Lord Christ who promises to be with us always. Be prepared to go wherever God will lead you. For at the end, there is indeed a promised land called the Kingdom of God.

105

Good Friday

Isaiah 52:13 — 53:12

This is the fourth and final Servant Song in Second Isaiah, and because of its content, it has been called the Suffering Servant Song. As with the Servant Song that we dealt with on Passion Sunday, it was originally a prophecy considering an idealized Israel. Second Isaiah set before the exiles in Babylonia the task of giving their life for the sake of the world. Israel was despised and rejected in exile, cursed by all who saw her plight. But there would come a time when God would deliver her from captivity and exalt her among the nations. When other peoples saw her salvation, then they would realize that God had subjected Israel to judgment in order that he might manifest his power to save her before all the world. Israel would become the living testimony to the God of judgment and of salvation, and by that testimony, all peoples would be led to worship the Lord.

That is the dialogue that is carried out in this song. The Lord speaks in 52:13-15. Then the foreign nations take up the speech in 53:1-10, and finally God ends the speech in 53:11-12. The foreigners are utterly amazed that the people whom they thought had been rejected by God were instead delivered by that God and raised on high. Israel was as good as dead in exile, and yet God gave her new life. Surely God must have had a purpose for doing such a thing, and the nations realize that Israel went through suffering and death for their sake, that they might be saved.

Second Isaiah is thus calling his people to a missionary task in this poem. But as in all the Old Testament, it is not the task of actively going forth into the world and proclaiming the ways of God. Rather, it is the task of being God's true servant, willing to submit to his will, even unto death. It is the task of truly being God's people, in order that the nations may see God's work in Israel and turn and worship the Lord.

107

If we were to translate that into our life, our God-given task as the church would be truly to be the church, so dedicated to the service of God that we would be willing to die in order to carry out God's will. We would be willing to give up everything — our money, our building, our programs, our reputation — if such sacrifice would further God's purpose of saving all peoples.

There have been Christians who have done that — Kagawa of Japan who gave his eyesight and finally his life to live among the poor of Japan; Mother Teresa who gave up all to take the dying off the streets of India and to comfort them with the love of God in their last days; Martin Luther King, Jr., who braved prison and scorn, police dogs and beatings to turn around the conscience of a nation; Albert Schweitzer who left a promising career as a musician and theologian to minister to the sick in the jungles of Africa; dozens of women and men who everywhere have given up this world's goods and status to serve Christ in slums and hospices, orphanages and storefront churches across the land. And yes, faithful mothers who spend hours with their disabled or retarded children, and faithful husbands who exhaust themselves in the care of a spouse with Alzheimer's. All have been suffering servants of their Lord, willing to surrender everything to serve him.

When you talk to such people, most of them are not joyless, however. Rather, their hope is in God, whom they know will finally say, "Well done, thou good and faithful servant. Inherit the kingdom prepared for you." And such persons are powerful witnesses to the workings of God, aren't they? Like the Suffering Servant drawing all nations to God, faithful souls draw others to him, to find the strength, the hope, the joy that so illumine their faithful lives.

There was One, however, who outdid us all in sacrifice and joy as the Suffering Servant. When the disciples and apostles and authors of the New Testament strained to tell who Jesus Christ is, they could do no other but describe his life and death and resurrection in terms of this Suffering Servant song.

Everywhere throughout the New Testament, the words of this song sound forth. Jesus is the one who gives his life as a ransom for many, says Mark (10:45) and who is silent before his oppressors at his trial (Mark 14:61). Jesus is reckoned with the transgressors, writes Luke (22:37), condemned as a criminal and hung on a cross between two thieves. He is like Second Isaiah's lamb that is led to the slaughter, in the Book of Acts (8:32), but he is the Lamb of God who takes away the sins of the world, in John (1:29). Jesus' grave is made with a rich man called Joseph of Arimathea (Matthew 27:57-60), yet certainly he had committed no sin and spoken no guile (1 Peter 2:22). And like the nations in the Suffering Servant Song, we have come to realize that our Lord is the one by whose stripes, whose whipping, we were healed when we had all gone astray like sheep (1 Peter 2:24-25).

The final, true servant of God is our Lord Jesus Christ. He became in his death what Israel was always meant to be. His trial and unjust sentence by Pilate, his death on the cross between two robbers, his burial in a borrowed grave fulfilled the words of our prophet. But we must remember why that death took place — to take upon himself our sins and to suffer the punishment we deserved from God for our evil ways.

On this Good Friday, perhaps we all should adopt the role of the foreign nations in our Servant Song, and confess with them that Jesus "was wounded for our transgressions, he was bruised for our iniquities; upon him was the chastisement that made us whole, and with his stripes we are healed" (Isaiah 53:5). Christ died in our place, taking upon himself our wrong. He gave his life for our sakes that we might not die. For "the wages of sin is death" (Romans 6:23), and you and I are sinners.

There was something else, however, that the foreigners realized, according to our passage. They came to understand that "it was the will of the Lord to bruise" the servant, and that it was God who had put the servant "to grief" (v. 10). It was God's will that our Lord Jesus die on the cross of Golgotha. Jesus had prayed in the Garden of Gethsemane that, if possible, he not go to the cross. But our Lord realized that such was the will of his Father. And so he gave up his life willingly, because that was the plan of his Father. Not because his God was some sort of abusing Father. Not because God desired vengeance and blood. Heaven help us if those are our thoughts! No, it was the will of God that his Son die on the cross, because God loves us and wants to save us. God took upon himself our sin in the person of his Son. God himself bore our iniquities instead of holding us accountable for them. And that was pure love and pure mercy extended to us by our heavenly Father. Surely, our only response can be the one that we sing in Isaac Watts' great hymn: "Love so amazing, so divine, demands my soul, my life, my all."

Easter Day

Acts 10:34-43

We have a crowd here today on this Easter Sunday. Churches are always crowded on Easter. As the prophet Isaiah would say, the multitudes literally trample the courts of God. And we are glad you all have come.

A lot of different reasons have led us here, of course. For those of us who worship regularly in this church, Easter Sunday is the crown and climax of the Christian year. For others, who do not come so often, Easter Sunday always brings with it special music, and some of you are music lovers. Others of you just like to witness the pageantry of the church on two Sundays in the year, on Easter and on Christmas. Those seem like special times. And then certainly there are a few here because they want to show off their new Easter clothes, joining the fashionable Easter parade. But maybe, too, this crowd has showed up because we all have the inkling that Easter bears with it some hope about that death we all have to face. Whatever your reasons for attending this morning, we are glad that you have come.

I cannot help thinking, however, that the crowd here this morning reminds me of the crowd that the Apostle Peter faced in Caesarea in our Old Testament lesson. Most of them were unknown to Peter, and what is more, they were Gentiles.

Peter had days before received a strange vision from the Lord in which a large sheet was lowered from heaven with all kinds of unclean animals upon it. And Peter, the strict Jew, had been commanded to eat that unclean food. Following that, a delegation of men, sent by one Cornelius, a Roman centurion, had shown up at Peter's house and told him that he should follow them to Cornelius' residence in Gentile territory. So Peter, not knowing exactly where he was going, followed and arrived in Caesarea. And there in Cornelius' house, Peter found an assembly of uncircumcised Gentiles waiting for him.

Moreover, they told him, "We are all here present in the sight of God, to hear all that you have been commanded by the Lord" (v. 33). In short, those Gentiles wanted to hear a sermon.

It was an amazing request of Peter, because that apostle had always preached to Jews throughout Jerusalem and Judea and Galilee, in strictly Jewish territory. The gospel had been sent to the Jews, and that was Peter's usual audience. And now he was being asked to preach to non-Jews and strangers, just as the church is asked every Easter to proclaim the gospel to outsiders and to those who do not regularly attend Christian worship.

It raises an interesting question, doesn't it? Is the gospel of Jesus Christ intended only for those inside the church, for those who come every Sunday and pay their pledge and take part in church activities? Is the gospel exclusive good news? Or is it intended to be spread throughout the earth?

There are some misguided souls who have tried to turn the Christian faith into an exclusive club, of course. "If you don't believe exactly what I believe," they say, "you don't belong. If you do those things of which I disapprove, you're not among the righteous. If you associate with that kind of people, you can't associate with us." Someone took a poll once in a particular denomination and found that three-fourths of the members of that church thought they would go to heaven. But they were sure that only one-fourth of their neighbors would. Such is our propensity to take upon ourselves the judgments that belong only to God and to shut out others from our exclusive club.

But Peter, in our Old Testament lesson, has learned differently. That strange vision that he had from God, the arrival of the delegation from Cornelius, and the eager faces of the Gentile crowd before him, convince him otherwise. "Truly, I perceive," he says, "that God shows no partiality."

God doesn't care a whit, you see, who you are or where you came from. He does not judge according to human standards. God sees our hearts. And those of us here this morning whose hearts are open to hear the gospel are accepted by God and counted among his flock. "I have other sheep who are not of this fold," Jesus told his Jewish listeners (John 10:16). And surely you and I and all of us Gentiles are numbered among those other sheep.

So what does Peter tell those foreigners who are gathered together in Cornelius' house? He tells them the simple story of Jesus of Nazareth. Jesus, in whom dwelt the Holy Spirit of God, Jesus who acted for God, went about all of Palestine doing good, says our text. He healed the sick and overcame evil spirits and taught about the will of God, preaching justice and the love of God and forgiveness for all who believed in him. But because the Jews were shocked when he claimed that he was from God, and because the Roman authorities were afraid when they saw so many following him, they crucified Jesus between two thieves on the hill of Golgotha.

But on the third day at dawn, when some women went to the tomb where Jesus had been buried, in order to anoint his dead body, they found the tomb empty. To the amazement of the disciples, then, Jesus appeared alive first to Mary Magdalene, but then to his disciples, who saw the wounds of the nails in his hands and the mark where the spear had been thrust in his side. After that, the Apostle Paul tells us that Jesus appeared alive to more than 500 people and to Paul himself. What is more, the risen Christ commissioned his disciples to go throughout all the world, and to tell the good news that he was risen. Because that good news, you see, means that our evil world cannot do Jesus Christ to death. And death itself has lost its sting and the grave has lost its victory. There is life eternal for all who trust Christ. There is the forgiveness of sins. And there is new life, a good way of living abundantly, right now on this earth.

Peter preached that sermon to those Gentiles, because he knew that Jesus Christ is Lord, not just of an exclusive little group, not Lord of just those whom we would choose, but Lord over all the earth, with all its multitudes of peoples. Jesus Christ is risen and reigns over earth and seas and skies. Death could not hold him fast, and our sinful ways and the ways of this sin-marked planet cannot defeat him. As Handel celebrated in the "Hallelujah Chorus," "The kingdoms of this world have become the kingdoms of our Lord and of his Christ, and he shall reign forever and ever, to the glory of God."

Our scripture lesson tells us that after the assembly in Cornelius' house heard Peter's sermon, the Holy Spirit descended upon them all, and they were baptized in the name of Jesus Christ. God, through the preaching of his gospel, offers the forgiveness, the new life, the eternal life, the victory of our Lord Jesus Christ, to all. To me, and to you — to all of you here this morning.

Second Sunday of Easter

Acts 5:27-32

"We must obey God rather than men" (Acts 5:29). That is the theme of our passage and, indeed, of this whole section of Acts, chapters 3-8. After the resurrection of Jesus, the Holy Spirit is sweeping through Jerusalem with power to enable Peter and John and the other followers of Jesus to heal, to convert multitudes, and to speak boldly. The result is that Jerusalem is in an uproar, and the disciples are repeatedly hauled before the Sanhedrin, the Jewish religious and political council, to account for what is happening.

Apparently the council or Sanhedrin (*synhedrion* in the Greek) was a rather fluid body, made up of those who happened to be in power as leaders of the community at the moment. In Acts, it consists of the high priest and his family members, various rulers, elders, scribes, Sadducees, and Pharisees. They act as a kind of judicial Supreme Court to interpret and guard Jewish life, custom, and law. It was the Sanhedrin that judged Jesus and delivered him over to Pilate (Matthew 26-27), and it is the Sanhedrin that examines and punishes the followers of Jesus for their teaching and activity.

The council has lots to do, according to Acts. First, Peter and John heal a man beside the Beautiful Gate in Jerusalem, a man who has been lame from birth for forty years. And Peter and John have to explain to the council and the onlookers by what power they have done this deed (Acts 3-4). Consequently, the council gives them orders "not to speak or teach at all in the name of Jesus" (Acts 4:17). The disciples go out and speak anyway, "with great power," giving "their testimony to the resurrection of the Lord Jesus" (Acts 4:33). In reaction, crowds of people hold the disciples in high esteem, multitudes are added to the followers of Jesus, and Jerusalem is flooded with sick people, all wanting to be healed, so many in fact that the streets are crowded with the beds and pallets of the lame and diseased (Acts 5:12-16). This time, the Sanhedrin doesn't hesitate. It throws the disciples into prison, only to find that an angel of the Lord opens the prison doors and sets them free, commanding them to go and stand in the temple and to speak to the people all the words of life (vv. 17-20). Once again the apostles are brought before the council, and that brings us to our text for the morning.

The high priest questions the Christians, as he questioned Jesus. The apostles were strictly charged not to teach in Christ's name, the high priest says, and now they have not only brought in the crowds to Jerusalem, but they have accused the council of killing Jesus. Rather than making excuses, Peter and the apostles renew that accusation and proclaim that nevertheless, God has exalted Jesus to the position of power on his right hand as Leader and Savior, giving forgiveness to Israel. This enrages the Sanhedrin, who want to sentence the apostles to death, but fortunately, a faithful Pharisee named Gamaliel intervenes and saves the apostles from being killed. They do not escape punishment entirely, however. They are beaten and then released, only to go on preaching and teaching (vv. 33-42). "We must obey God rather than men," the apostles have said (v. 29), and so nothing can stop their witnessing for the Lord.

The passage affords many pertinent thoughts for us. First of all, it is quite clear that religious bureaucrats may be wrong. The church receives lots of directions from the "higher ups" in its structure these days, and those directions may be wise, or they may be unwise. The question is: How to judge them? Should the directions of church executives be followed, or should they be ignored?

The question becomes even more pressing, however, when we consider how many religious movements there are today in our society. The multitude of sects and religious groups in this country now numbers in the thousands. And most of them have a charismatic leader of some sort who is saying, "Follow me." Some of the groups seem to be very fine. Promise Keepers, Young Life, Youth for Christ, and similar movements have seemed to further the cause of Christ in this country. But there are others that have enslaved their followers. The Moonies, for example, think they have a new messiah in the person of Sun Myung Moon. Jim Jones lured a whole colony to their death, as did the leader of Heaven's Gate. Louis Farrakhan sometimes preached a message of racial and religious hatred.

Many parents have agonized over the entrance of their son or daughter into some cult or sect, and some have gone to extreme measures to try to free their children from the effects of such groups, hiring persons to de-program the young person and to bring him or her back into normal life. Maybe some family members tried equally to de-program their relatives from the early Christian movement. After all, Acts tells us that the Christians in Jerusalem lived together in a commune, sharing all their goods in common or selling them and distributing the proceeds to any who were in need (Acts 2:44-45). There were undoubtedly Jews who thought the Christians' lifestyle was crazy. Equally, as we have seen, the religious authorities tried to prevent the spread of the gospel and to warn others away from Jesus' followers.

So how do we judge between legitimate religious groups and illegitimate? When do we listen to those religious "higher-ups" who warn us and our family members from being led astray by some charismatic leader or other?

There are probably two good criteria for judgment. First, what is the leader of the group claiming for him- or herself? Are they claiming absolute authority? Or in humility and selflessness, are they directing our commitment to God? No human being is to have absolute authority over another in the Christian faith. The kingdom and the power and the glory belong to God alone, and any leader who seeks rule and honor for him- or herself is not serving the Lord.

Second, what God does the message of the group proclaim? The human imagination is very fertile, and persons dream up all sorts of deities these days. But is the God being proclaimed the God and Father of our Lord Jesus Christ? Is he the God who raised Jesus Christ from the dead? The early Christians in Jerusalem had experienced the risen Christ. They had talked and eaten with him, and they knew that only the true God could raise Jesus from the grave and make him Lord. So is that the God whom some group is proclaiming, or are they worshiping another?

117

The scriptures give two basic identifications of God. In the Old Testament, God is the one who delivered Israel out of Egypt, out of the house of bondage. In the New Testament, the same God is the one who raised Jesus Christ from the dead. Only the God who has done those acts is truly Lord. And he commands us, "You shall have no other gods besides me" (Exodus 20:3). If we hold on to that command and those identifying acts, and worship and serve that Lord, we shall not be led astray by false prophets and illegitimate gurus.

Third Sunday of Easter

Acts 9:1-6 (7-20)

We have three different accounts of the conversion of Saul in the Gospel according to Luke (9:1-20; 22:6-16; 26:12-18). They differ in a few minor details, but essentially they are the same. In addition, Paul writes of his conversion in Galatians 1:11-16, and in 1 Corinthians 9:1 and 15:8-9, stating that at the time of his conversion on the road to Damascus, he saw the Lord. For Paul, that made him an apostle, equal to the twelve. An apostle, in Paul's thought, was one who had seen the risen Christ and had been sent to announce that good news. No mention is made of seeing the Lord in Luke's account, and for Luke, the only apostles were the twelve in Jerusalem who had been with the Lord during his life on earth. Luke always wanted to exalt the importance of the Jerusalem church.

Despite these differences, both Luke and Paul himself record that in the vicinity of Damascus, Paul underwent a life-transforming experience, which changed him from Saul, the persecutor of the early Christians, to Paul, the Christian apostle to the Gentile world. The story in Luke stands in the middle of a series of conversion accounts of the Samaritans and of the Ethiopian eunuch in chapter 8 and of those converted by Peter in 9:32-42. The Spirit is moving mightily, out into the world. Certainly, however, the conversion of Saul is seen as the paradigmatic account.

The story of Saul is the story of an enemy of Christ. Saul hated Christians. He hunted them down and had them flogged and expelled from the synagogue (contrary to Luke's notice that Saul delivered them to Jerusalem). And because Saul hated Christians, he also hated Christ. That's what Jesus is saying in Matthew 25:40: "Truly, I say to you, as you did it to one of the least of these my brethren, you did it to me." Paul was a strict Pharisee, and according to the teaching of the law, anyone who hung on a tree was cursed by God (Deuteronomy 21:23). Yet Christians were proclaiming that the Messiah himself had been condemned by the law and crucified on a tree. Moreover, they were maintaining that the law had been fulfilled and was at an end. That was too much for Pharisee Saul.

It has been the common stereotype to say that Saul was converted because he could not follow the law and that he finally realized that he could be saved only by grace. But that theory has no basis in fact. Paul himself states that as to righteousness, he was blameless under the law (Philippians 3:6). Paul could follow the law to the letter. It was not his own spiritual or psychological inner state that led to his conversion. We should give up that thought.

Indeed, Paul's story shows us rather clearly that we do not convert ourselves. There is nothing that we can do to transform our own lives. As the prophet Jeremiah once stated, "Can the Ethiopian change his skin or the leopard his spots? Then also you can do good who are accustomed to do evil" (Jeremiah 13:23). We cannot transform ourselves, because everything we do is tainted by our sin, and the more we rely only on ourselves, rather than on God, the farther we fall into sin.

Rather, we are converted to faith and our lives are transformed solely by the grace of God, by his active intervention in our hearts and minds. And that is what happened to Saul. He had heard about Jesus. He was present at the stoning of Stephen, and he knew what Christians were preaching. But suddenly Jesus himself confronted Saul on that Damascus road. A great light flashed around Saul from the sky, and he heard a voice call his name, "Saul, Saul, why do you persecute me?" When Saul asked whose voice it was, Jesus identified himself, told Saul to get up, and to enter Damascus. But Saul was struck blind and had to be led by his companions.

In short, Saul the zealot, a Hebrew of Hebrews, the Pharisaic fulfiller of the law, the active, energetic persecutor who could hunt down Christians to punish them — that proud and vigorous man was suddenly helpless, needing to be led along like a little child and then unable to eat or drink for three days.

I wonder if that is not what happens to us when we truly become Christians, that we lose all reliance on ourselves and become solely dependent on the guiding of God. We too are an energetic, goal-oriented people, aren't we? We set our plans and arrange our schedules and work hard to fulfill our own desires and to reach our own goals. And then the risen Lord Christ intervenes in our lives and somehow our plans and goals become secondary. And what we really desire is to further God's purpose of love and to serve his will in the world. As John the Baptist said, we decrease and Christ increases (John 3:30), and the Lord takes over our lives. And we find, as a converted Paul found, that it is not we who live, but Christ who lives in us (Galatians 3:20).

That does not necessarily happen to us suddenly as it happened to Saul. We need not undergo a sudden conversion experience like Saul's to be taken into the Christian life. Some of us are raised in Christian homes, by truly devout parents, and we are nurtured and brought up in the faith, day by day and year by year, until our dependence on Christ becomes our way of life, and we become true servants of the Lord.

One thing is certain, however. Christ does not redeem us from our old life and from our old self for no purpose. In our text, when Ananias hesitates to go to Saul and lay his hands upon him, Ananias is told by the Lord, "Go, for he is a chosen instrument of mine to carry my name before the Gentiles and kings and the sons of Israel" (v. 15). Saul, who became Paul, was chosen by God for a task.

That is the way with all of the servants of the Lord in the Bible. Elijah, in the Old Testament, hearing the still, small voice of God on Mount Horeb, was not allowed to bask in the experience. Instead he was commanded to return to his people and to start a revolution (1 Kings 19). And Peter, James, and John at the Transfiguration were not allowed to build booths on the mountain and to continue to enjoy the mystical vision. Instead, they had to go down and follow their Master to Jerusalem and to a cross.

So it is too with us. God has not transformed our lives by his active Spirit and made us his disciples just so we can enjoy his fellowship all by ourselves. And surely he has not made us Christians so we, in our pride, can claim some sort of spiritual superiority to those around us. Heaven help us if we exchange our discipleship for self-glorification, For then we do not belong to Christ, and he is not our Lord. No, we are called to accomplish tasks for our Lord. Each one of us has a task.

Yet, in fulfilling the purpose for which God converted us, we may even have to suffer. God says in our text that he "will show (Paul) how much he must suffer for the sake of (his) name" (v. 16). And Paul, in giving his litany of his past, tells how true that became. He says he was five times beaten with forty lashes, three times with rods; once stoned, three times shipwrecked, a night and a day adrift at sea, always on a journey and always in danger for the sake of his Lord (2 Corinthians 11:24-29). But he could also say, these slight momentary afflictions are "preparing for us an eternal weight of glory beyond all comparison" (2 Corinthians 4:17). And so he could advise his churches to "rejoice in the Lord always; again I will say, Rejoice" (Philippians 4:4). Our discipleship, our conversions by the grace of God, our service in his name, lead to glory, good Christians, and to rejoicing.

Fourth Sunday of Easter

Acts 9:36-43

A number of subsidiary themes emerge in this reading from Acts, and we probably should take note of them, although they do not form the main thrust of the text.

We have here a brief story of a Hebrew woman given the Aramaic name of Tabitha, which means "gazelle," or called Dorcas in the Greek. This is the only mention that we have of Dorcas in the scripture, but over the centuries, her reputation as a person of good works and charity toward the poor has been preserved. It is now not unusual to find "Dorcas societies" in some local churches made up of women dedicated to similar good deeds. Dorcas' service in the cause of Christ has lasted far beyond her own lifetime.

Dorcas, in our text, falls ill and dies, leaving behind her a whole group of poor widows to whom she has ministered and for whom she has provided clothing and support. Widows in Israel were among the destitute, having no one to protect them or to furnish them the necessities of life. Thus, there are repeated admonitions in the Old Testament to show mercy toward widows, orphans, and strangers, and Dorcas is an example of that mercy.

But now Dorcas is dead, and the poor widows, whom she has helped, weep in grief, not knowing what will become of them or to whom to turn. Their grief is overcome with joy when Peter raises Dorcas from the dead and presents her alive to the bystanders and church in Joppa. The result is that many in Joppa, who do not belong to the church there, are converted to faith in the Lord. Once again, Luke, the writer of Acts, is presenting us with the on-going power of the Spirit that is rapidly converting the Mediterranean world.

One of the subsidiary themes of the text is certainly Peter's willingness to leave Lydda and immediately to accompany the two men to Joppa to the upper room where the body of Dorcas has been washed and prepared for burial. Joppa is located at about the midpoint of the sea coast of Palestine. Lydda is some ten miles inland, and the journey between them was probably made on foot. But Peter showed no hesitation in going.

I have known of pastors who have been reluctant to go immediately to the side of someone who has lost a loved one or to show up at a hospital when a parishioner is going to undergo surgery. And some deacons, elders, laity only reluctantly minister personally to someone in need or in an emergency. But Peter goes immediately when he is summoned. What the Christians in Joppa expected of him is not told us. But they obviously thought he could do something to aid in the situation.

What Peter actually does, of course, is totally astounding. Like Elisha in the Old Testament (2 Kings 4:32-35) and like Jesus in the Gospel according to John (John 11:38-44), Peter raises Dorcas from the dead. It is not our role as preachers and hearers of the Word of God to question or doubt the event. We are not to make up fanciful theories, supposing that Dorcas was not really dead but in a coma. Nor are we to take the account as a pious exaggeration. No. The story is simply there, and Luke expects us to accept it as an actual event.

Indeed, in Matthew, Jesus tells the twelve disciples that they will be able to do such deeds. When he sends the Twelve out on a mission to "the lost sheep of the house of Israel," our Lord tells them, "Preach as you go, saying, 'The Kingdom of Heaven is at hand,' " and then he commands, "Heal the sick, raise the dead, cleanse lepers, cast out demons" (Matthew 10:7-8). Jesus fully expects his disciples to be able to do such things. It is not up to us to ridicule his expectation.

Another subsidiary theme is the place of good works and charity in the life of the church. Dorcas is a model of Christian service, and her enduring reputation is justly earned. But of course we do not do good deeds and minister to the poor and help the needy to earn a reputation, do we? Some persons do, of course. They minister to others because it will bring glory to themselves. Our Lord would say, as he said to those who ostentatiously practice their piety, "Truly, I say to you, they have their reward" (Matthew 6:2), namely, the admiration of their fellows.

But it is God's reward that has any worth at all, and we do not earn that reward by our good works. Rather, his gifts to us of his forgiveness and eternal life are gifts solely of his grace and mercy. We do not earn our salvation. As Jesus taught, when we have done all that is commanded us by God, nevertheless, we are still unworthy servants; we have only done what is our duty (Luke 17:10). None of us earns our way into heaven. God gives us heaven simply out of his overflowing love.

But what, finally, is the main point of this passage from Acts? It is that Peter's healing of Dorcas shows forth the power of the Kingdom of God that has come near to us in Jesus Christ. We note in the story that Peter does not have such power in himself. Before he raises Dorcas from death, Peter kneels down and prays. He does not have any ability in himself to defeat the power of death. Jesus said as much when he sent those twelve disciples out on that mission in Matthew that I mentioned. He told them first of all, "Preach as you go, saying, 'The kingdom of Heaven is at hand' " (Matthew 10:7).

The Kingdom of God has drawn near to us in the person of our Lord — the kingdom with all its power for good and its eternal life. In our Gospel lesson, Jesus tells us that he gives his sheep his eternal life, and they shall never perish, and no one shall snatch them out of his hand (John 10:28). It is by that power, and that power alone, that Peter is able to raise Dorcas.

In this text, we have a foretaste of that heavenly scene in our Epistle lesson in Revelation, when those who have died for the sake of the gospel are with Christ, the Lamb of God. And they participate in springs of living water, and God wipes every tear from their eyes (Revelation 7:17). And as Revelation later says, death is no more, and mourning and crying and pain have passed away, for the Kingdom of God has come to earth (Revelation 21:4).

So our text for the morning is promissory, you see. You and I, no matter how strong our faith, cannot raise the dead as Peter did. Peter works within the circle of that power that has been lent to the twelve disciples by the risen Christ. And Peter's resurrection of Dorcas is an exhibition of that power. But Peter's act in Christ is also a promise to us — that such is the kingdom toward which we journey, when death shall be no more. God in our Lord Jesus Christ defeated the powers of death on Easter morn, and to all who trust him, he will give the gift of everlasting life with God.

Fifth Sunday of Easter

Acts 11:1-18

This story about Peter's mission to the Gentiles continues the account that began in 10:1, and it repeats in greater detail the content of Peter's vision that was already mentioned in 10:9-16. It is a remarkable story, because it treats rather lightly a dispute that was widespread in the New Testament church, the dispute over conditions to be laid upon Gentile converts to the faith.

The apostles and disciples of Jesus, who were the earliest Christians, were originally Jews, and some of them, at least, continued to obey some of the stipulations of Jewish law. For example, Peter, in our text, had not before eaten any animals that were listed in the Torah as unclean (cf. Leviticus ch. 11). In addition, these early Jewish Christians were circumcised, according to Jewish law (cf. Genesis 17:9-14). As Gentiles began coming into the early church, the question therefore arose as to whether or not they too had to be circumcised and follow table laws.

The Apostle Paul was quite sure that following the Jewish law was no longer incumbent upon any Christians, because when Christians tried to follow the law, they were depending on themselves, whereas salvation depended entirely on faith in God's work in Jesus Christ. Thus, Paul's whole letter to the church at Galatia strongly condemns those who insist on the necessity of keeping Judaism's law. "If anyone is preaching to you a different gospel," Paul writes, "let him be accursed" (Galatians 1:9). And Paul's letter to the Romans emphasizes that Jews have no advantage over Gentiles. In Acts 15, however, a circumcision party led by James, insists that Gentile Christians follow Jewish dietary restrictions, a decision with which Peter and Barnabas later agree, infuriating Paul (Galatians 2:11-14. For a full historical account, see Paul J. Achtemeier, *The Quest for Unity in the New Testament Church*).

In our text for the morning, however, Peter has not yet given in to the circumcision party. He has allowed Gentiles into the table fellowship of the church (perhaps meaning the Lord's Supper) (v. 3), and he has baptized uncircumcised Gentiles into the faith (Acts 10:47-48). The Jews who are members of the circumcision party in Jerusalem therefore require Peter to explain his actions. At this point Peter repeats the account of the vision that he has received from God, and he testifies that God has given the gift of the Holy Spirit to the Gentiles, who are then baptized. Therefore, Peter says, "Who was I that I could withstand God?" (v. 17).

We applaud Peter's action, because we don't have many requirements for joining the church these days, do we? Almost anyone can belong. To be sure, some churches have Inquirers' Classes, in which they try to given some education in the Christian faith to those seeking membership. A few pastors lay rather strenuous requirements upon seekers: join a class that meets weekly at 7:30 a.m.; practice the daily discipline of prayer and Bible study; exhibit a Christian lifestyle. But on the whole, it is very easy to join the church, and most churches are out there begging for members, trying to sell their program like another product on the market. All you need is a perfunctory confession of faith in Jesus and you're in. So, from such a standpoint, why wouldn't Peter accept the Gentile converts? Everyone should be accepted.

On the other hand, within the church, those who have been members for a long time often have the attitude that the circumcision party had in our text. They don't want to let people in of whom *they* disapprove. How can Mr. So-and-So be a church member; he drinks and smokes. That woman certainly shouldn't be in our circle; she had a divorce, and now she's running around with another man. That guy is actually on welfare; that woman wears that short, revealing dress; that man was very rude to me the other day; they certainly don't act like Christians ought to act. There are a lot of people on whom we would like to impose our rules, aren't there? And so we would fit in very well with the circumcision party.

In fact, we probably would have a hard time accepting Jesus, just like the Pharisees did. With whom did he associate? With all of those lawbreakers and social subversives. He even said sinners and prostitutes would get into the kingdom before us. We too would probably want to crucify him for the offense he was.

But Peter's statement is a good corrective for us. "Who was I that I could withstand God?" God, you see, chooses people whom we would never choose. He's always surprising that way. He does not go by the rules of the politically correct and the socially acceptable. He singles out that long-haired youth in the rock group or that confessed criminal in jail; he touches the life of a struggling single mother or the heart of a timid, middle-aged spinster. And he pours out his Holy Spirit upon them and claims them for his purpose. They show up at our church door, wanting to sit at the Lord's table with us, and we, unless we belong to that circumcision party, receive them as God has already done. For who are we that we can withstand God?

The membership of the Christian Church is all God's doing. Have you noticed that in our readings in Acts? It was God who sent his Holy Spirit on the Gentiles and converted them to the faith. It was God who changed a Saul into Paul, and who converted a Roman centurion named Cornelius, just as he changed that Ethiopian eunuch to whom Philip preached, and that multitude on the day of Pentecost. God is at work through his Holy Spirit, multiplying his faithful throughout the world. And that action of God of which we read in Acts is still going on today. God is on the move, advancing toward his kingdom, and in all of our difficulties and sufferings, we need to keep that in mind.

Let us say two more things about those who are converted in the stories of the Acts of the Apostles. First of all, they are converted into the church. Entering the Christian life is not an individualistic occurrence. Rather, all of those early Jewish and Gentile Christians of whom we read in Acts, immediately were incorporated into a fellowship. No one is ever a Christian all by him- or herself. Rather, they join a company of people and are called to live the Christian life within that company — loving one another, serving one another, caring each for the other. When we become a Christian, we are called to love God, but we are equally called to love our neighbor, and that neighbor, first of all, is in the church. As Paul writes, "As we have opportunity, let us do good to all ...

129

but especially to those who are of the household of faith" (Galatians 6:10).

Second, conversion to the Christian faith and into the church is never an end in itself. God does not send his Holy Spirit to convert us, and then that's the total sum of his action. No. God converts us to a new way of life. We repent and literally "turn around." And then we walk, we walk in a new direction, guided and strengthened always for God's purpose for us. God has made us Christians in order to do a task for him in his world. And our conversion is only the beginning of that life-long task. By the mercy of God in Jesus Christ, he has poured out his Holy Spirit upon us and made us Christians. We have been converted and baptized and now we set out on a journey, working all along the way to serve and to glorify our Savior.

Sixth Sunday of Easter

Acts 16:9-15

Our text for the morning sets us down in the middle of what many have called Paul's second missionary journey. Luke schematizes Paul's travels and arranges them so that Paul goes on three journeys, returning twice to the "headquarters" of the church in Jerusalem. Paul's letters, on the other hand, give a somewhat different account. But it is certain that Paul traveled thousands of miles for Christ in his mission to the Gentiles.

As we pick up our story, Paul, accompanied by Silas, journeys through Syria and Cilicia, visiting various local congregations and strengthening them in the faith (15:41). At Lystra, in Asia Minor, Timothy joins them in their travels (16:1-3). He is an appropriate Christian companion, because his mother is Jewish and his father is Greek, an apt symbol of the gospel intended for both Jew and Gentile.

That which is emphasized in our text, however, is the fact that Paul's journeys are entirely guided by the Holy Spirit. The little group of travelers want to go into Asia Minor (Phrygia and Galatia, 16:6), but the Holy Spirit forbids them from diverting there to preach. Similarly, they try to go into Bithynia, also in Asia Minor, and once again, the "Spirit of Jesus" does not allow them to do so (16:7). Finally, while they are at Troas, on the northwest corner of Asia Minor, Paul is given a vision of a man standing and beseeching him, "Come over to Macedonia and help us" (16:9). So in obedience to the vision, Paul and his companions set sail from Troas, land briefly at Samothrace, go on to Neapolis, and finally arrive at Philippi, an important Roman colony on the eastern border of Macedonia. They have traveled over 2,000 miles, and all along the way, the Holy Spirit has shown them where to go.

In the Gospel lesson for the day from John 14:23-29, and indeed, throughout chapters 14-16 in the Fourth Gospel, which tell

131

of the Last Supper, Jesus promises his disciples that he will never leave them desolate, that he will come to them in the Spirit, and teach them, and defend them. In fact, it is through the work of the Holy Spirit that Jesus will continue his work on earth (John 16:8-11). In writing Acts, Luke is very conscious of that gift. It is the Holy Spirit that guides Paul on his journeys, that brings conversions, and that opens the heart of Lydia to receive Paul's words and to be baptized in Philippi (16:14). Christian disciples and missionaries never go it alone. They are accompanied and led and strengthened by Christ's continuing work through his Spirit. And you and I can be sure that Christ is with us in his Spirit, if we are faithful.

Some persons have claimed in our time that they have received new revelations from the Spirit. But always we must remember that the Spirit never speaks contrary to Christ. Thus, if a revelation is given, we must always ask, does it accord with Christ? Is it his Spirit that has spoken or been revealed, or is it an alien spirit? Paul and his companions are led by Christ, still at work, as they journey through the Mediterranean world.

We sometimes wonder why God chose Paul's period in history to convert the Mediterranean world. But it has often been remarked that Paul's journeys were made considerably easier by the magnificent system of Romans roads throughout that empire. God takes advantage of all sorts of human constructions to advance his kingdom.

If you are an alert reader or listener, you have noticed that at 16:11-17, the story is told using "we" (also in 20:5-15; 21:1-18; 27:1—28:16). That sounds as if a companion of Paul, perhaps Timothy or Silas, is writing the account of their journey. Perhaps they are, although the style is no different than that found in the rest of Acts. But the "we" accounts certainly give us the impression that these are real stories of actual happenings in the first century A.D. And you can believe that they are. Paul has arrived at Philippi, and he founds the church there, so that later he writes the letter to them that we now call Philippians. Some people have the idea that the Bible is a fairy tale, or some imaginative story that ancient authors have dreamed up. No, indeed. The Bible tells the story of flesh and blood people, who have been met, transformed, and set on tasks for the living God who has acted in their lives.

One of those people in our text is Lydia, a rather wealthy woman, who is a seller of valuable purple goods, made from the extraction of sea shells. She is a worshiper of God, our passage tells us, and she has gathered with a number of other pious women at a place beside the river, where the women meet for prayer. The text does not say to what god the women are praying. The Romans had lots of gods, and the devotion of the women might have been to any one of those pagan deities. On the other hand, perhaps Lydia had already heard of Christ and was praying to the Father. She had not yet, however, become a member of the church. But God opened Lydia's heart to give heed to what Paul was saying (v. 14), and she and her household joined the Christian community by being baptized by Paul. The Christian faith is a communal affair; it involves incorporation into a body of believers. And Lydia joins that body when she is baptized, just as we join it at our baptisms. As we said last Sunday, you cannot be a Christian all by yourself.

This brief story of Lydia is remarkable for two things, however. First, it involves the baptism of a wealthy woman. The gospel is not meant just for the poor. God's preference for the poor has perhaps been over-emphasized in our time. But just as the gospel is meant for both Jew and Gentile, so it is meant for both poor and rich. In the Old Testament, Amos was a wealthy landowner, Isaiah was welcomed in the court of kings. In the New Testament, the rich tax collector Zacchaeus becomes the object of Christ's salvation (Luke 19:1-10), and Luke tells us that wealthy women supported the mission of Jesus and his disciples out of their own pockets (Luke 8:3). To be sure, wealth is given to be used wisely in the service of others. "Everyone to whom much is given, of him will much be required" (Luke 12:48). But the good news of Jesus Christ is given to rich and poor alike. We have only to receive it.

Second, this story of Lydia is remarkable because her husband is not mentioned, she is the head of her household, and she is a woman. We have all too often ignored the important place of women in the New Testament church. Lydia here is the founder and leader of the church in her house, just as Prisca or Priscilla, with her husband who is mentioned second, is the leader of a household church in Rome (Romans 16:3). The first witness of the resurrection and therefore the first apostle was a woman, Mary Magdalene, according to John (John 20:11-18). And in Luke, it is the faithful women, who remained at the cross when the other disciples deserted Jesus, and who first discovered that Jesus' tomb was empty (Luke 24:1-12).

Women played an important part as supporters and leaders of the church in the spread of the gospel in the first century. And only an age that has never understood the good news of Christ can relegate them to second class citizenship in the church. Paul declared that in Christ there is neither Jew nor Greek, neither slave nor free, neither male nor female (Galatians 3:28). The ancient split between male and female, which led to the subjugation of women (Genesis 3:16), has been overcome in our Lord. And in his travels, as recorded in Acts, Paul is a witness to that fact.

Ascension of Our Lord

Acts 1:1-11

As we all know, the book of the Acts of the Apostles forms the second volume, as it were, of Luke's writing. In the Gospel, he has told the account of Jesus' birth, life, death, and resurrection. Now he begins the account of the growth of the early church by the power of the Holy Spirit.

To begin his second volume, however, Luke repeats some of the things he has said at the end of the Gospel story. Once again, the command to the disciples to remain in Jerusalem until they receive God's promised "power from on high" in the form of the Holy Spirit is given (Luke 24:49; Acts 1:4). Once again the apostles are told that they are to be Christ's witnesses in Jerusalem, Judea, Samaria, and to the ends of the earth (Luke 24:48; Acts 1:8). Once again Christ's resurrection appearances are told, although Acts, accounting for the passage of time, mentions many more appearances than does the Gospel. And once again, the fact that the risen Christ ascends into heaven is stated (Luke 24:51; Acts 1:10). It's as if the author wants to doubly impress all of these facts on our minds.

But then the writer includes some new content in this text for the morning. First of all, he tells about the apostles asking that question of Jesus before the Lord ascends into heaven: "Lord, will you at this time restore the kingdom to Israel?" (v. 6). Israel's expectation throughout the Old Testament history was that God would finally come to establish his kingdom on earth. At that time, "in that day" as the Old Testament repeatedly puts it, all the enemies of God would be done away and the faithful in Israel would be exalted as inhabitants of the Kingdom of God. It was a question concerning when God would bring human history to an end and usher in his rule over all the earth.

Similarly, Acts 1:10 recounts the appearance of the two men in white, who are angels, to the apostles, after Jesus has ascended. "Men of Galilee," the angels ask the disciples, "why do you stand looking into heaven?" (v. 11). Then the angels give the promise of Christ's second coming. "This Jesus, who was taken up from you into heaven, will come in the same way as you saw him go into heaven."

In adding these additions to his account, it is as if Luke knows all of our questioning and gives answers to it. For some persons spend a lot of time, standing around, trying to figure out the date of the Lord's second coming. There have been countless times in human history when some so-called prophet has decided that such and such a date will mark the time when the final cataclysm takes place and the Lord Christ will come again. I'm sure you all have read newspaper accounts of such people. They sell all their goods and go out and stand on a hill top, gazing into heaven, looking for Christ's appearance. Indeed, when the year 2000 drew near, many people believed that would mark God's final battle with his enemies, the end of human history, and the coming of the Kingdom of God on earth.

But to such speculation, the risen Christ replies, "It is not for you to know the times and the seasons which the Father has fixed by his own authority" (v. 7). We do not know when Christ will come again or when God will establish his kingdom on earth. Jesus said that repeatedly in the Gospel stories. "Of that day or that hour no one knows," Jesus taught, "not even the angels in heaven, nor the Son, but only the Father" (Mark 13:32 and parallels). Jesus himself did not know the time, and if people claim that they do, they are saying that they know more than our Lord knows. Thus, Jesus' command to us is "Watch!" Be prepared in faith for his coming again.

That's not the only question we have, however. We wonder what does it mean when Luke says that Jesus ascended into heaven. Is heaven up in the sky somewhere? Such a conception doesn't fit our scientific age. How could Christ ascend to the Father? Where is the Father? Indeed, was Jesus really raised from the dead? Did the apostles actually see him, or was that just some kind of psychological experience that they had after they mourned his death? And so on and on go our questions. We become like those apostles, standing and gazing up into heaven and wondering what it all means. And the angels' question in our text becomes the question addressed to us. "Why are you standing around, gazing into heaven, wondering, doubting, when there is a job to do?"

The good news is very clear, and we recite that good news every time we confess the Apostles' Creed. "I believe in Jesus Christ, his only Son, our Lord; who was conceived by the Holy Ghost, born of the virgin Mary, suffered under Pontius Pilate, was crucified, dead, and buried. On the third day he rose again from the dead. He ascended into heaven and sitteth on the right hand of God the Father. From thence he shall come to judge the quick and the dead."

Jesus Christ has ascended to the Father. And so he is no longer limited by geography, by flesh, by time, and by space. No. Now he enjoys a universal rule over all people from the right hand of God's power. All authority in heaven and on earth has been given to him, he told us (Matthew 28:18). Now he has authority to rule over your sins and to forgive them and to do away with them. Now he has the power to defeat the forces of evil and death in your life and to give you eternal life. Now he has the love to send his Spirit into your hearts and to transform you and to make you a new person from the inside out. Now he can give you the fruits of his Spirit: love, joy, peace, patience, kindness, goodness and faithfulness, gentleness and self-control (Galatians 5:22-23), so that you have true life and have it abundantly.

The main point of our text, therefore, is that we are witnesses of all these things. We have not been called into the Christian faith as disciples of our Lord to stand around and to engage in idle speculation. Rather, we have been called to tell about our new life in Christ to all the persons around us, and in fact, to the ends of the earth. We are called to go into all the world and to make disciples, baptizing them in the name of the Father and the Son and the Holy Spirit, and teaching them to observe all that Jesus has commanded us. We are called by the way we live our lives and by the way we speak to testify in our homes and in our society and in our world that Jesus Christ is ascended to the Father and now reigns as Lord over all. We are summoned to all of that, so that finally every knee will willingly bow and every tongue will joyfully confess that Jesus Christ is Lord, to the glory of God the Father. And then when the end does come, good Christians, our Lord will be able to say to us, "Well done, thou good and faithful servant. Enter into the kingdom prepared for you."

Pentecost

Acts 2:1-21

This reading from Acts is the stated lesson in all three cycles of the lectionary. The preacher may therefore want to consult the expositions in Cycles A and B also.

In our first lesson for last Sunday, just before his ascension into heaven, the risen Christ commanded his disciples to remain in Jerusalem and to wait until they were clothed with power from on high (Luke 24:49) by the gift of the Holy Spirit to them (Acts 1:8). Only then would the disciples be equipped with the power and ability to be Christ's "witnesses in Jerusalem and in all Judea and Samaria and to the end of the earth" (Acts 1:8). Our text for this Sunday now records the Day of Pentecost, when the Holy Spirit came upon them.

We often make the mistake of speaking of God's Spirit as a beautiful, ethereal feeling that is given to us in quietness and peace. But if you have ever heard Bach's presentation of the Holy Spirit in his *B-Minor Mass*, you know that the Spirit comes with great energy. Bach's chorus is full of rapid, staccato notes that sweep on toward their climax in powerful sounds. The Holy Spirit of God is no quiet ghost. It is power, energy, transforming might from the almighty God of the resurrection.

So it is too in our text for the morning. The Spirit rushes upon the gathered disciples like a mighty wind that whirls about in the whole room (v. 2). It brings with it flames of fire — always a symbol of God's presence in the scriptures — that divide and rest on the head of each of the disciples. The Spirit transforms their speech, so that suddenly they can speak in the language of Mesopotamia and Palestine, Asia Minor and Egypt, Rome and Crete and Arabia. And it prompts the disciples to tell of "the mighty works of God," in all of those languages (v. 11), so that travelers from all those lands can understand what is being said.

Several major themes thrust out at us from this text. First of all, it is clear that God keeps his promises. His Christ had promised the disciples at the Last Supper that he would not leave them desolate, but that he would come to them in the Person of the Holy Spirit as their Advocate, Counselor, and Teacher (John chs. 14-16). Further, the risen Christ had promised the apostles that they would be clothed with the power of the Spirit from on high. Here now, at Pentecost, the Son of God keeps those promises, as he always keeps his promises. We can count on that. We modern Christian disciples of our Lord are never left on our own, dependent on our own abilities and power to spread the gospel. Rather, God in Christ grants us the gift of himself in the third person of the Trinity, in the Person of the Holy Spirit, and he is with us to the end of the age, as he promised he would be (Matthew 28:20), empowering us also to be his witnesses to the end of the earth.

Where do we receive that Spirit of Christ? Usually not in a pentecostal experience like that given to the first disciples. Rather, the Holy Spirit is granted to us first in our baptisms, and then repeatedly it is poured out upon us through the sacrament of the Lord's Supper and through the Word of the gospel when that is truly preached from the pulpit. Every Christian is a recipient of the Holy Spirit. That is the gift that has made us Christians, and apart from that Spirit, we cannot lead a Christian life or be Christ's faithful disciples. "Apart from me, you can do nothing," Jesus taught us (John 15:5), and he comes to us in the Spirit.

Second, in the whole sweep of the Bible's history, it is clear that when the disciples are enabled to speak in the languages of all their Mediterranean world, the judgment that fell on all nations at the Tower of Babel has been reversed. In the story of Babel, in Genesis 11, which is actually the story of us all, God confused the languages of all peoples and scattered them abroad on the earth, as a judgment on their pride and attempts to run their own lives. In short, all forms of human community became impossible, because there was no understanding any more between husband and wife, brother and brother, society and society, nation and nation (the story of Genesis 3-11). And that is true, isn't it? We can't get along with one another anymore. We are constantly at odds with one another, in our homes or in our communities or in the world at large, filling our lives with angers and violence, misunderstandings and wars.

But now, suddenly at Pentecost, all the various people understand one another. Their language is no more confused. They hear as one company the mighty acts of God. And it is the gift of the Holy Spirit that makes that understanding possible.

Is that not the story of the Christian mission, that wherever the gospel is told in the love and power of the Spirit, controversies are healed, barriers of race and gender and nationality are overcome, and persons are enabled to live in harmony and peace with one another? Certainly that Spirit has healed many broken marriages and united many disrupted communities and enabled black and white and red and yellow to be bound together in "one great fellowship of love" in the church "throughout the whole wide earth." The Holy Spirit is a power to heal all of our broken relationships.

Third, in his sermon explaining what is happening to the gathered company at Pentecost, Peter quotes the words of the prophet Joel, verses 17-21 (Joel 2:28-32). Back in the fifth century B.C., Joel had declared what would happen "in the last days," that is, at the time when God would come to put down his enemies and to usher in his kingdom over all the earth. Shortly before that time, Joel proclaimed, there would be a mighty outpouring of the Spirit "on all flesh," so that all ranks of persons would be able to speak the Word of God, as the prophets of old had spoken it. That was what was happening there in that room at Pentecost, Peter explained. The Spirit was being given to all.

In short, a new age was beginning. The coming of the Kingdom of God was being prepared. Jesus Christ had embodied in his person the powers of that kingdom (cf. Mark 1:15; Luke 11:20), and now by the gift of his Spirit to the disciples, that power was spreading through all the world. God was beginning to usher in his final rule over all the earth. His final coming would be ushered in by "wonders in the heaven above and signs on the earth beneath" (v. 19), but before that time, the gospel was to be preached, so that all who believed and called on the name of the Lord would be saved, in the final judgment, for eternal life in the Kingdom of God (v. 21).

Can you believe that, that there is now the power of the King-dom of God let loose in this world by Christ's Spirit, that you and I stand at the beginning of the new age of the kingdom, and that by our words and living we can spread a gospel that can bring eternal life to every person on earth? That's our situation, good Christians. God's kingdom is coming on earth, even as it is in heaven. You and I have been granted his Holy Spirit to empower us to spread the Word. And our mission, given us by the Spirit, can mean eternal life or death to everyone who observes our living or who hears our words from God. Pentecost has been called the birthday of the church. But it is not like every other birthday party. It is our call to be the witnesses of God's new age, that all persons whom he loves, and whom we are to love, may become participants in his everlast-ing kingdom.

Trinity Sunday

Proverbs 8:1-4, 22-31

Perhaps no doctrine of the Christian Church is more obscure in the minds of church-goers than is the doctrine of the Trinity, the fact that God is One in three Persons. The early church councils of the fourth and fifth centuries A.D. debated long and hard before they arrived at a satisfactory statement of the doctrine, and still today, persons misunderstand or distort the teaching.

The doctrine of the Trinity took shape out of the testimony of the scriptures, beginning with their witness to Jesus Christ. Most of the writers of the New Testament were originally Jews who believed in one God. But when the apostles and disciples encountered Jesus of Nazareth and witnessed his life, death, and resurrection, they became convinced that he was fully Immanuel, God with them, the Person of God incarnated in human flesh. After Christ's resurrection and ascension, the apostles and disciples also found that God in Christ continued fully to be with them in the Person of the Holy Spirit, as Christ has promised. Thus, the one God of the Old Testament was fully present in the Father, the Son, and the Holy Spirit. He was One, in three Persons. Not only the Father, but also the Son and the Holy Spirit, are wholly divine, the Son also having been fully human and incarnated in human flesh in Jesus of Nazareth. The Son who is with us is God. The Holy Spirit who comes to us is God. They are not lesser deities than the Father, and to all of them, Father, Son, or Holy Spirit, we pray and give our adoration.

It is rather strange, therefore, that the lectionary for this Sunday of the Trinity designates a passage about Wisdom from the Old Testament, as if Wisdom is somehow a Person in the Trinity.

The figure of Wisdom in our text for the morning is personified as a female figure. She calls to human beings to listen to her and to learn her teachings (vv. 1-5). She is described as the product of God's first act of creation (v. 22), and she says she was present when God made all of the rest of the universe (vv. 23-30). God rejoiced in her (v. 30), and she rejoiced in God's creation of the world and of human beings (v. 31).

On the basis of this text, many persons in our time have therefore claimed that Wisdom is a divine figure, and we have abroad in our society what has come to be called Sophia worship, Sophia being the Greek translation of Wisdom. Principally such Sophia worship has appealed to radical feminists, because Sophia or Wisdom is a female figure, and they do not wish to say that a male, namely Jesus Christ, is their Savior and Redeemer. So for many such radical feminists, the worship of Sophia has replaced the worship of our Lord Jesus Christ.

Such Sophia-worshipers find their deity in all of creation, in, through, under all things, as a kind of spirit pervading the universe. She is identified with the vital forces in the natural world and even with sexual drives in human beings. Thus, at the Re-imagining conference of 1993, a conference that since has been repeated every year, Sophia was prayed to in these words:

> *Sophia, creator god, let your milk and honey flow ...*
> *Our sweet Sophia, we are women in your image. With*
> *nectar between our thighs, we invite a lover, we birth a*
> *child. With our warm body fluids, we remind the world*
> *of its pleasures and sensations ... We celebrate our*
> *bodiliness, our physicality, the sensations of pleasure,*
> *our oneness with earth and water.*
> From tapes of the conference, Tape 12-1, Side B

We need to call such worship by its proper name, however. It is idolatry, because you and I worship the one God who has commanded us, "You shall have no other gods besides me" (Exodus 20:3; cf. Mark 10:17-20). He has revealed himself to us in his incarnation in Jesus Christ, and he continues to be our God and to be with us in the Person of the Holy Spirit, who is given to us from the Father and the Son.

So how, then, are we to understand this text from the Old Testament about Wisdom? This personified figure of Wisdom in Proverbs 8 will probably become clear for us if we understand Wisdom in the Old Testament (and indeed in the apocryphal book of Wisdom) as the *plan* of God. Wisdom was there with God when he made the universes, the fifty billion galaxies that our astronomers tell us they have discovered through their telescopes. God had a plan when he created all things and persons. And he delighted in his plan, because he wanted to make a creation that was "very good" (Genesis 1:31).

On the basis of this text from Proverbs, you and I can celebrate God's good plan — how he brought forth the rivers and raised up the mountains; how he laid out the fields with their good earth, and how he established the deeps of the seas; how he brought order out of chaos and made a world of delight and beauty and fruitfulness, that you and I were given to enjoy.

We can, however, also realize how often we distort God's plan for a good world, how readily we trash our environment and how sinfully we distort the loving relationships in which he has set us; how blindly we have turned his abundant life into darkness and death for ourselves and all things.

But the scriptures have something else to say about God's wisdom, about his plan for his world. In the New Testament, who becomes identified with the wisdom of God and in fact replaces all which that female figure does in the Old Testament? Jesus Christ. "Christ Jesus," Paul writes, "whom God made our wisdom, our righteousness and sanctification and redemption" (1 Corinthians 1:30). Christ is the wisdom of God, and in him is found the truth of God (John 14:6). Moreover, the eternal plan of God is to unite all things in Christ (Ephesians 1:10).

So through Christ, God has made all things (John 1:3) and according to Christ, he orders all things. According to his love in Christ Jesus, God loves his world. According to the teachings of Christ, God calls and instructs all people. According to the forgiveness of Christ, God forgives and redeems his world. According to his purpose in Christ our Lord, God will save his world.

There is no other name under heaven given to us by which we may be saved than the name of Jesus Christ our Lord (Acts 4:12). Sophia is not our God. Jesus Christ is our God, the one through whom the Father in his mercy revealed himself, and the one with whom he sends his Holy Spirit always to be with us.

Proper 6

1 Kings 21:1-21a

Israel in the Old Testament and the Christian Church are both understood in the scriptures to be the covenant people of God. As such, both of them are called by God to be his "holy nation" (Exodus 19:6; 1 Peter 2:9). To be "holy," according to the Bible, does not mean to be morally pure, however. Rather it means to be "set apart" for God's purposes. Both Israel and the church, having entered into covenant with God, are God's "set-apart" people. As the ancient oracle of Balaam puts it, Israel is "a people dwelling alone, and not reckoning itself among the nations" (Numbers 23:9). And as the Apostle Paul writes to the church, "Do not be conformed to this world" (Romans 12:2).

So Israel and the church, as God's holy people, are to live differently from the society around them, and they are to see situations and events differently than other people see them (cf. Leviticus 18:1-4). They live differently and they see differently, because they obey God and not human beings.

For example, a Christian does not follow the customs of society in marriage. One out of two marriages in our time ends up in divorce court; a Christian promises before God to love, cherish, and honor his or her mate "until death doth us part." In the same fashion, a Christian does not do just what "comes naturally." It is not natural to love your enemies and to pray for those who persecute you. A Christian does not view other persons as our power-ridden, materialistic society views the poor or the weak. A Christian understands that the meek shall inherit the earth and that God blesses the poor. Christians are a covenant, set-apart people, called to live according to God's will and not the will or desires of the world around them.

It is this quality of being set apart that we confront in the story of Naboth's vineyard in 1 Kings 21. Naboth is a poor peasant who

147

has inherited a little plot of land that happens to lie next to the royal holdings of the evil King Ahab, who ruled the northern kingdom of Israel from about 869 to 850 B.C. Kings never have enough property, they think, so Ahab offers to buy Naboth's little vineyard. He even offers Naboth a fair price for the plot of earth. But that square of dirt represents Naboth's share in God's land promised to his covenant people. Naboth inherited it from his family. It was the gift of God to his forbears and to him. It represents Naboth's participation in God's gracious gift of the promised land. Naboth too is a recipient of God's fulfillment of his promise of land to Abraham. So Naboth will not sell the land, not even to the king. And Ahab understands Naboth's reason. After all, Ahab too is an Israelite, so he understands Naboth's refusal even if he does not like it. And Ahab sulks, like some disappointed child.

Ahab's wife, Jezebel, however, is a different breed. She's not a set-apart person; she's a Phoenician princess, a worshiper of the pagan god Baal and a persistent enemy of Israel's prophets and religion. God's promise of the land means nothing to her. She lives by the ways of the world. Power is her motto, and kings should have power. So she cynically uses Israel's own covenant law to bring about the death of Naboth. She pays two false witnesses to accuse Naboth of cursing God and king (cf. Exodus 22:28), because two witnesses of a crime were necessary according to the law (Deuteronomy 17:6; 19:15) and cursing God was a capital offense, bringing death by stoning (Leviticus 24:16).

That which covenant people know, but which Jezebel does not understand, is that there is a higher Power than that of state or king or society. Covenant people are sworn to obey that Power, but they also know that all people are responsible to him, for they know that the final King over this earth is God, and God holds all persons accountable. The result is that Elijah, the prophet of God, condemns Ahab and his dynasty to destruction, and Jezebel to death, a gruesome death that comes upon her after the dynasty has fallen (2 Kings 9-10). Our Lord of the covenant, who is the Lord of our universe, is not mocked (cf. Galatians 6:7), and those who defy him are destroyed.

That would be a terrible sentence for us all, wouldn't it, for what one of us has not disobeyed the will of our God and followed the ways of the world? "The wages of sin is death," writes Paul (Romans 6:23), and all of us deserve that death. But because of his wondrous mercy, God also pours out upon us, not only his judgment of death, but finally also his grace in Jesus Christ.

Lutheran Option:
2 Samuel 11:26 — 12:10, 13-15

In the story of his sin with Bathsheba, King David, who ruled over Israel from 1000 to 961 B.C., experienced a measure of God's grace. Kings in Israel were subject to the covenant law of God (cf. Deuteronomy 17:18-20), and that law was summarized in the Ten Commandments: "You shall not kill. You shall not commit adultery. You shall not steal. You shall not bear false witness. You shall not covet ... your neighbor's wife" (Exodus 20:13-17). Because of his unholy lust for Bathsheba, the wife of Uriah the Hittite, the great king David of Israel broke every one of those basic laws of God.

The prophet Nathan confronted David with his sin in what was a masterful sermon. After arousing David's anger with the story of the rich man who stole the poor man's little lamb, Nathan whirled on David and accused him, "You are the man!" David deserved death for his lustful coveting and adultery with Bathsheba, for his robbery of her, for his deceitfulness and finally murder of Uriah. And David recognizes his sin (2 Samuel 12:13); that is at least a first step in his repentance. But sin does not go unpunished by God, and it always has its consequences. David does not die, but the child he has fathered by Bathsheba does die for David's sin, and that undoubtedly added to David's remorse. When we repent of sin, our eyes are often opened to see the terrible consequences we have brought on others by our sinful conduct.

Nevertheless, David continues on the throne, but that continuance is solely a gift of God's grace. David does not deserve to continue to rule Israel. He is an adulterer and a murderer, and if we read his story in 2 Samuel, we find that he is also a terrible father to his sons. Nevertheless, by the grace of God, his rule becomes the greatest in Israel's history, and he becomes the forerunner of the davidic Messiah.

But David too, like Ahab later, is subject to the rule of God. The power of the state is not greater than that of God's power. And the power of any individual cannot loose them from their responsibility to the one God who rules over all the affairs of earth. God's judgment but indeed, also, God's grace are supreme in this world of ours. They were supreme over the lives of Ahab and David, and they are supreme over ours.

We are God's covenant people, sworn to trust and obey him in all the affairs of our lives, sworn to live by his will and not by the will of our sinful society. We therefore are not to trust finally governments or human ways or customs of the society around us. We are called to trust and obey God above all other demands. But the only thing that makes that possible for us is finally the mercy of God, shown to us in our Lord Jesus Christ. In Christ we find forgiveness for our errant lives. Because of him we are condemned not to death for our sin, but are given the gift of eternal life. Finally the action of God toward us sinners is one of over-ruling and undeserved mercy. And the God of the covenant, though he will not be mocked, is above all, the God of love. Surely, such astounding love calls forth our love and obedience in return.

Proper 7

1 Kings 19:1-15a

This story follows immediately on Elijah's victory over Jezebel's prophets of Baal on Mount Carmel, in 1 Kings 18:20-40. Queen Jezebel of the northern kingdom is so angry with Elijah for slaying the prophets of Baal that she vows to kill him, and Elijah flees for his life. Many sermons from this passage have concentrated on the manner of revelation to Elijah and on the "still, small voice" of God that comes to him. Probably the emphasis of the passage, however, is on Elijah and his discouragement over his prophetic office. As such, the passage can be used to deal with our dejections and despair as Christian disciples.

It is not easy to lead a Christian life or even a reasonably good life in our present society. As the prophet Habakkuk mourned, "The wicked surround the righteous, so justice goes forth perverted" (Habakkuk 1:4). The power of evil in our time seems to be so strong that no action or program seems to prevail against it. We pour billions into our public schools only to have two-thirds of our high school graduates end up illiterate. We declare a "war on poverty," but the welfare rolls never end. We send military troops into trouble spots abroad to try to establish peaceful communities, but ethnic wars and terrorists remain and young men seem to have died in vain. We try to end world hunger, but millions still starve from malnutrition.

Even on a personal level, our Christian efforts seem sometimes to produce no fruit. As one of our neighbors voiced it, "We raise up our kids, and someone else tears them down." Or we pour every thought and energy we have into a marriage, and yet it crumbles and we are left alone. Sometimes an effort at forgiveness brings forth only scorn and deeper enmity. Or good actions are misinterpreted and misunderstood. As for prayer, sometimes we can pray and pray and yet see no result of our pleading. It can lead us to despair of maintaining our Christian ways, even as Elijah despaired of continuing his prophetic office.

Elijah was scared for his life, and he fled southward into the desert. His journey was his attempt to flee his office and to forget the past. Indeed, Elijah's flight was an attempt to escape his life altogether. "Take away my life," he prayed to God. He literally wanted to die. His mission seemed hopeless. His prophecy seemed empty. His faithful actions seemed futile.

Elijah learned, however, that he was not on his own journey, but rather on a journey for God. Twice God's angels fed him food in the wilderness, and strengthened his will to go to Mount Horeb, that mountain sometimes called Sinai, where God had first appeared to Israel.

When Elijah arrived at the mountain, moreover, how did God deal with Elijah's despair? Did the Lord sympathize with his frightened prophet and understand Elijah was a victim? Were the Lord's ministrations to his prophet full of tenderness and comfort, accommodating to Elijah's need? No, the Lord approached Elijah, preceded by wind and earthquake and fire — all the accustomed manifestations of God's presence on earth. And then God spoke to Elijah, first in a question that awoke Elijah to his responsibility. "What are you doing here, Elijah, when you should be back prophesying in Israel?" And when Elijah pleaded his case, the Lord did not sympathize. Instead he told Elijah to go back to work. Indeed, he told Elijah to start a revolution that would finally topple the dynasty of Ahab. But at the end, in verse 18, the Lord also assured Elijah he was not alone in his faith. There were still 7,000 faithful Israelites in Israel who had not bowed down to the pagan Baal.

Responsibility, command to return and work, assurance that our Christian efforts are not in vain. Thus does God deal with our discouragement when we grow dejected about our Christian lives. We are not on our own life-journeys, as the disciples of Jesus Christ. We are on God's journey, and the end result is in his hands. You and I are called simply to continue to be faithful.

Lutheran Option: Isaiah 65:1-9

This passage, which is a judgment oracle and which actually ends with verse 7, is a reply to the long lament in 63:7—64:12. The passage that follows in 65:8-25 is an oracle of salvation.

For the first time in the Old Testament, the congregation of post-exilic Israel is divided into two groups in God's eyes, and God levels his judgment against only the evil-doers in the community. Previously the community was judged or saved as one. Now God differentiates between those who do good and those who do evil (vv. 8-9).

The Lord spells out why he is bringing his judgment on the evil-doers in Israel. They have repeatedly walked in their own way rather than according to the commandments of God. They have provoked the one Lord by their idolatrous worship practices, sacrificing in the "gardens" of the Canaanite high places (v. 3); engaging in the worship of the dead (v. 4); eating those foods that were Canaanite totem animals and therefore forbidden to Israel (v. 4). Indeed, even the Zadokite priests who were set apart as "holy" to the Lord have practiced such evil ways, and so they will be subject to the fire of God's wrath (v. 5). Previously, the people had complained about the silence of God (64:12). Now God will not keep silent in the face of Israel's sin (v. 6).

It is a passage that should prompt us to ask whether or not we are worshiping the one Father of our Lord Jesus Christ or whether we have devoted ourselves to the worship of other gods — our own welfare, our success, our accumulation of things, our bodies, our families, or all of those alien gods and goddesses like Sophia and the New Age gurus that are found in so many other religions today.

Most prominent in the passage, however, are its opening lines. God has repeatedly revealed himself to his people and pleaded with them to return to him, like a loving Father calling for his son. "Here am I," he has called, "here am I." That summons is one of overwhelming mercy, for God cannot be found by us unless he reveals himself to us. The Christian faith is a revealed religion, and unless God approaches us, we do not know who he is, and we cannot go to him.

But God has revealed himself to us. Throughout the history of Israel and supremely in the life, death, and resurrection of Jesus Christ God has made himself known to us and drawn near to us and called out, "Here am I." And his loving desire, then, has been that we hear his call and follow after him, committing our hearts and lives to his ways in obedience to his commandments.

Indeed, God's very name in the Old Testament — Yahweh — embodies that call of "Here am I." The name means "the one who is indeed with you" (Exodus 3:14), just as we are told in the New Testament that Jesus Christ is "Immanuel," God with us.

"Here am I," God calls to each one of us and to this congregation assembled here this morning. "Here am I," waiting for your surrender, waiting for your worship, waiting for the commitment of your lives, so that you walk in my ways and love me and trust me with all your days and years. For I will give you abundant life and the riches of Christ beyond imagining, and finally eternal life with me in my kingdom of love and good and peace.

God is here, calling. And he waits for our answer.

Proper 8

2 Kings 2:1-2, 6-14

This is one of those texts that remains almost totally incomprehensible to the congregation when it is read on this Sunday of the church year. It therefore requires a good deal of explanation.

The ministry of Elijah is about to end. Even so great a servant of the Lord comes to the end of his labors, as the end comes to all of us. But Elijah, unlike the rest of us, will not experience death. Rather he will be "translated" or taken up immediately into heaven, as was our Lord at the time of his ascension.

Right there, of course, we have entered the realm of mystery, for we earth-bound human beings, made of the dust to which we return, know nothing of such a translation. And in fact, mystery permeates this whole account.

First of all, Elijah tries to rid himself of the company of Elisha, as if Elijah were withdrawing into another realm. When Elisha faithfully refuses to leave his teacher, Elijah leads Elisha on what seems a rather senseless journey, from Gilgal to Jericho, which is only a few miles from Gilgal, and then to the Jordan. At each place, they are met by "sons of the prophets," that is, by groups of those prophetic bands that lived together in colonies at the time. They warn Elisha of his teacher's departure, but are forbidden to speak of it further (vv. 4-5).

When Elijah and his pupil reach the Jordan, Elijah strikes the water with his mantle, and the two pass through on dry land, at which point, Elisha asks for a double share of Elijah's spirit. It is not a request to be greater than his master, however. Rather, Elisha is asking for the inheritance that was given a first-born son by his father (Deuteronomy 21:17). But he will receive such a gift only if he sees Elijah as he is being taken up into heaven. Suddenly there appear a chariot of fire and horses of fire between the two, and Elijah is lifted up into heaven by a whirlwind, whereupon Elisha cries out that strange phrase, "My father, my father! The chariots of Israel and its horsemen!" Elisha is left the mantle of Elijah by which he too can strike the waters of the Jordan and pass back through on dry land. Elisha has become Elijah's prophetic successor, possessing his same powerful spirit of prophecy.

What does it all mean? Those fiery chariots and horses in the vision are symbols of the unseen power of God (cf. 2 Kings 6:15-18; 7:6-7). And that power has been concentrated in the prophetic Word that Elijah spoke and that will now be spoken by Elisha. Elijah's word was as powerful as a heavenly army, because it was the Word of the Lord.

Behind all of this story and behind our lives and the world around us, this text testifies to the fact that there is an unseen realm of God that constantly is influencing the course of affairs on our earth. God is at work, shaping events in our lives, sending forth his power to achieve his purposes on earth. And much of that power is concentrated now in the word that God speaks to us.

We do not receive that word from prophets like Elijah or Elisha any more. Rather, now God's word comes to us through the scriptures, written and preached. The word was incarnated in Jesus Christ our Lord, and now through the scriptural testimony to him, God's power works in our hearts and lives. It is a power greater than all the powers of earth, and it is symbolized in our text by those fiery chariots and horses. It is a power that transforms lives and heals broken spirits and overcomes the forces of evil and death. And that power works right now in the midst of this gathered congregation.

Is there anything, then, that you and I have to fear? Are we fearful of the future? God is at work. Do we wonder how evil can be overcome? God's victory is sure. Do we fear death and the valley of the shadow? God's incarnate word in Christ triumphed over death. The God of the prophets Elijah and Elisha, and the Father of our Lord Jesus Christ, is the God of power, but also supremely the God of love. And he now encircles your life and mine. And so when you are afraid and anxious, despairing and afflicted in this world, remember the unseen world of God, and those fiery chariots and horses, and cry out to your Father in heaven, as Elisha cried, for in him is your sure salvation.

Lutheran Option: 1 Kings 19:15-16, 19-21

When the prophet Elijah was met by God on Mount Horeb and given God's command to get to work (see the preceding Sunday's lesson), one of the commands given to him was to return and anoint Elisha as a prophet in his place (v. 16). Verses 19-21 in this text now portray Elijah's obedience to that command.

Elisha is a very rich man in this story. He is plowing his field with twelve yoke of oxen, a team that stands in sharp contrast to the poor man's solitary yoked ox. But God's will has a way of interrupting the lives of all sorts of people, rich and poor, renowned and obscure, talented and unaccomplished. Let no one in any station of life think God has no role for them in his purpose.

God also has a way of interrupting our lives unexpectedly. Elisha is going about his business, when suddenly Elijah throws his prophetic mantle over Elisha's shoulders. There is no word before this that suggests Elisha expected such a thing.

But Elisha knows what the gesture means. He is called to be Elijah's disciple; he is called to leave all and follow, much like those disciples of Jesus were called to leave their fishing nets and to follow after him. It is a call to an unknown future. The disciples of our Lord did not know that Golgotha awaited them. And Elisha does not know on what course Elijah will lead him.

As an obedient son who honors his father and his mother, however, Elisha asks that he be allowed to say goodbye to his parents. And Elijah respects that request. The fact that Jesus denies such a wish, according to our Gospel lesson, shows the radical nature of our Lord's call to each one of us. But Elijah lets Elisha go back and say farewell. He gives him an admonition, however, in verse 20. That verse should be read, "Go back again, but remember what I have done to you." Remember now that you have been called to a higher loyalty than that which you owe your family, and indeed, that is what Jesus tells each one of us also. Our commitment to him and his kingdom is not to be hedged by any reservation on our part.

Elisha shows that he has no such reservation. There is no notice in our text that he does in fact go home to say goodbye to his parents. Rather, he simply goes back to his oxen that have been standing in the field, kills them, and distributes their meat to others. In short, he makes an absolute break with his past. He sheds his trappings of wealth and follows after Elijah to serve him in his prophetic calling.

Most of us are not called to leave our homes and families and familiar surroundings to follow after Jesus, although there are Christian missionaries who have done exactly that. But most of us are called to a new way of life in the place wherever God has put us. And there is to be no hedging in that call. We cannot dally occasionally in some sin of the past, which our Lord has shown us to be contrary to his will. We cannot retain old hatreds and grudges, when Christ has called us to a life of forgiveness. We cannot continue to ignore persons whom we thought were insignificant, when we now know as Christians that every person is loved in God's sight. We cannot continue to believe that our desires, our thoughts, our habits are supreme, when we have accepted Jesus Christ as our Lord. And surely, we cannot continue to lead lifestyles of conspicuous consumption when we have turned over everything we are and have to God.

The call to a Christian life is a radical call, as the call to the life of prophecy was a radical call to Elisha. It is a call that gives us an entirely new perspective on everything we have and are. But it is a call that gives back a thousand-fold for everything that we leave behind. Above all, it is a call to become what we were meant to be — servants of our Lord Jesus Christ and witnesses of his gospel. There is no higher calling in this world, nor does any life give our living more meaning. To serve in the name of Jesus Christ — there is no greater joy.

Proper 9

2 Kings 5:1-14

This story forms part of the Elisha cycle that is found in 2 Kings 2-13, and that is interspersed with stories of northern Israel's battle with Moab and of her continuing warfare with Syria. It is set in the ninth century B.C. during the reign of King Jehoram (849-842 B.C.) of Israel. As is true of most of the stories of the prophet Elisha, it concerns Elisha's pastoral, prophetic care for all persons, even for a commander of Israel's foe, Syria. Indeed, there is no more pastoral figure in the Old Testament than Elisha.

The story is simple and straightforward. Naaman is a "great man" of war, in favor with his king and country, "because by him the Lord has given victory to Syria" (v. 1). In short, Naaman's success is due to God's working. The Bible never abandons its view that the rise and fall of nations are due to the action of the Lord.

Naaman, however, is a leper. But his wife hears from her little Israelite slave-girl, who was captured in war, that the prophet Elisha could heal the leprosy (vv. 2-3). When Naaman tells this to his king, Ben-Hadad, the latter allows Naaman to travel to Samaria, bearing an enormous gift and a letter to the Israelite king, Jehoram. Jehoram has no power to cure leprosy, however. He knows that only God can heal or kill (cf. Deuteronomy 32:39). Therefore he is furious, thinking that Naaman's arrival signals a plot to attack Israel (vv. 4-7).

At this point, Elisha intervenes with Jehoram and bids him to send Naaman to him, so that Naaman "may know that there is a prophet in Israel" (v. 8) — so that Naaman may find out that the power of God works through his prophet. Always God has a hand in this story.

Naaman arrives with great fanfare, with his horses and chariots, at Elisha's door. He expects Elisha to make an elaborate ceremony of his cleansing, calling on the Lord to heal him (cf. v. 11).

159

But Elisha does not even personally appear. Instead he just sends out his servant to tell Naaman to wash in the Jordan River seven times in order to be cleansed of his leprosy.

This time Naaman is furious. Elisha has not recognized what a great man Naaman is and has not given him the attention due to one of his status. He departs in a rage, muttering that he could have washed in the rivers of Damascus if that is all it takes to cure leprosy (v. 12).

Once again, lowly servants become God's instrument, urging Naaman to humble himself and to wash in the Jordan. His rage gone, Naaman goes to the river and dips himself seven times, according to the word of Elisha, and his leprosy is healed (vv. 13-14).

Naaman had to get rid of himself. Humanly speaking, he was a very important person, full of pride in his own achievements, and expectant of proper deference shown to him. But the Lord pays no attention to the status and fame and image that we human beings think to achieve for ourselves. Indeed, the Gospel tells us that "whoever exalts himself will be humbled, and whoever humbles himself will be exalted" (Matthew 23:12, paraphrased). And both the Epistle and Gospel lesson bear that truth. "If anyone thinks he is something, when he is nothing, he deceives himself," reads Galatians (6:3). "Do not rejoice that the (evil) spirits are subject to you," Jesus teaches the seventy disciples, "but rejoice that your names are written in heaven" (Luke 10:20). It is not our human status that is important, but how we stand with God. And God works his will through little slave-girls and servants, and comes to those who are of a broken, contrite heart and spirit (Psalm 51:17; 34:18) — to those who know they have no goodness in themselves but who are totally reliant on their Lord. So our Lord Jesus commands us, "Take up your cross and follow me" (Mark 8:34). In other words, let yourself be crucified — your will, your desires, your plans — and submit yourself to the will of Christ Jesus, who can in truth make us all clean and whole again.

Lutheran Option: Isaiah 66:10-14

These verses constitute a portion of the long poem of Isaiah 66:1-18a, in which a number of brief oracles alternate between announcements of salvation for Jerusalem and judgment upon God's enemies, both within and without the holy city. Isaiah 66:10-13 is actually one stanza; verse 14 belongs to the salvation-judgment oracle in verses 14-17. The lectionary, however, has kept the salvation verses all together.

The reading comes from Trito-Isaiah (Isaiah 56-66), that was assembled by the Levitical priests in Jerusalem sometime after those in Babylonian exile had returned following Cyrus II's decree of 538 B.C.

The poem is addressed to those who "love" Jerusalem and who have mourned over her devastation at the hands of Babylonia (v. 1). But the mourning has also been over the sin that still is present in Zion (cf. e.g. Isaiah 64:5-7; 65:1-7). Third Isaiah is one of the few books in the Old Testament that separates out the faithful from the whole of Israel and announces salvation for them alone. There is now in this book an elect company within Israel's community that will alone experience God's future consolations.

Jerusalem is pictured in the figure of a mother, who will be comforted (cf. Isaiah 40:1), and who will give comfort to her faithful children. Those who love her will be able to nurse fully and deeply at her overflowing breast, which is her "glory" (v. 11). Shalom will flow out to her like a river (cf. Isaiah 48:18), increased by a stream of wealth from the nations round about. Her children will be carried on her hip and dandled upon her knees — both pictures of joy. For like a mother comforts her child, the Lord will comfort the faithful in Jerusalem (vv. 12-13). God will be the one who gives salvation to the holy city.

The faithful will therefore rejoice in their hearts and their vitality ("bones") will flourish like new grass (v. 14). And when the whole world sees the salvation of the faithful, it will know that the Lord saves his "servants" (cf. 65:8, 9, 13-15), and that he has lifted his hand in wrath against his enemies (v. 14). The revelation is intended as a universal witness to God's saving and judging work.

It would be difficult to know what to preach from this passage were it not for the fact that we now apply the title of Zion or Jerusalem to the Christian Church. The church has always called itself "Zion," as in several hymns. But Paul tells us also that faithful Christians belong to the "Jerusalem above" that "is free," and that "she is our mother" (Galatians 4:26). And Hebrews announces that we have come to "the city of the living God, the heavenly Jerusalem ... and to Jesus, the mediator of a new covenant" (Hebrews 12:22, 24).

If that be the case, certainly the church shares the characteristics of the Jerusalem described in Third Isaiah. It is full of sinful ways and often fails to seek the Lord (Isaiah 65:1). But there is also found in almost every congregation a little company of the faithful, who mourn over the state of the church because they love the church and her Lord, and who attempt to walk every day in the path of trust and obedience to God. It is to that faithful company that this good news of Third Isaiah is announced. God is going to make his church, his Jerusalem, new again. She will flourish and rejoice. More than that, John of Patmos tells us that there will be a new Jerusalem, a new church, a new people of God (Revelation 21:2), with whom God himself will dwell. And there will be no night, no wrong, no death and evil there, for God will have done away with them all.

Proper 10

Amos 7:7-17

This text gives the third in a series of four visions (7:1—8:3) that the prophet Amos was granted during the reign of Jeroboam II (787/6-747/6) in northern Israel. The series is interrupted by Amos' confrontation with the high priest Amaziah at the king's sanctuary in Bethel (7:10-17). In the first two visions (7:1-3, 4-6), Amos turned aside God's judgment on Israel by fulfilling the prophetic function of interceding for his faithless people.

Now the Lord tells Amos that he can no longer pass over Israel's flagrant sins of injustice and idolatry. The Lord has set a mason's plumb line in the midst of Israel, and that covenant people is no longer upright and straight. Measured by the commandments and will of God for justice in society and sincere worship from her heart, Israel has become crooked, veering sharply from her obedience of and trust in the Lord.

Israel, like the church, was the people of God who pledged to worship him and to honor his will alone. But during the "boom time" of Jeroboam II's reign, commerce flourished to produce a growing wealthy class that enjoyed luxury (cf. 3:15; 6:4) at the expense of the poor. Often the poor were cheated in the marketplace (8:5) or denied justice in the lay courts at the city gates (cf. 2:7; 5:10, 12). Unable to pay their debts, the poor peasants were thrown into prison or subjected to slavery (2:6; 8:4, 6). As the structures of society gradually broke down, debauchery increased (cf. 2:7-8; 6:5-6), while the consciences of the rich were placated by participation in an elaborate cultus (4:4-5; 5:21-23). At the same time, the leading class thought to find security behind strong military fortifications (6:8-11, 12-14).

God will put up with disobedience and evil only so long, however. He is a God of unfailing love, to be sure, who is slow to anger and patient in forgiveness. He repeatedly warns his covenant people of the consequences of their sin, through prophets and various calamities (cf. 4:6-11). But when the people will not listen and persist on a course that hinders God's good purpose for his world, God will not overlook their threat to his lordship.

The Lord therefore tells Amos that by an unnamed conqueror (cf. 6:14), he will pass through the midst of Israel, destroying their phony worship, their unjust community, and their government. The "high places," the local worship sites throughout the countryside, will become desolate of people, because the people will have been carried into exile. The "sanctuaries" of both Bethel and Dan, where Jeroboam I erected golden calves to be worshiped, will be laid waste. And the monarchy will fall victim to the "sword" of the Lord.

Amos' words have now become a threat to the government. Not only has Amos' prophecy attacked the state cult, but it has also spoken treason against the crown. The priest Amaziah, who is in charge of the royal sanctuary at Bethel, therefore sends a message to the king in the palace in Samaria, some fifty miles away, to report what Amos has been preaching (vv. 10-11). "Thus *Amos* has said," he reports. He does not believe Israel will go into exile or that Jeroboam will fall by the sword, because he does not believe Amos is speaking the Word of God.

Amaziah does not wait for the king's reply. He personally tries to banish Amos from the royal sanctuary. Go back to Judah, he orders, and prophesy there. Amaziah does not care if Amos preaches, because Amaziah does not believe the words of the prophecy. But he does not want such subversive words said at the king's place of worship, where they are likely to cause an uprising against the throne.

Amos, however, defends his ministry. I am not a professional prophet, he says, and I am not a member of a prophetic guild — such is the import of verse 14. But "the Lord took me ..." (v. 15). Amos is under a divine compulsion; he has to preach. His words are truly the Word of the Lord. But because Amaziah has not believed that Word, Amaziah's children will fall by the sword when Israel is invaded, his wife will become a harlot for the conquering soldiers, Israel's land will be divided as a spoil, and Amaziah himself will be carried into exile, where he will die. In 721 B.C., therefore, northern Israel falls to the troops of Assyria, her population is carried into exile and disappears from history, while her land is given to foreigners, known later as the "Samaritans."

God, who is "of purer eyes than to behold evil" (Habakkuk 1:13) will not allow evil to persist forever in his world. When the poor are trampled in the dust while the rich luxuriate in the *vita dolce*, when the worship of God becomes a mockery and his covenant people rely on everything and everyone but him, God speaks his Word, a Word that is now given us through the scriptures. And that Word is a powerful, effective force that shapes the course of history until it is fulfilled (cf. Isaiah 55:10-11; 1 Corinthians 1:18, 24). Such is the message of Amos that we must hear and ponder.

Lutheran Option: Deuteronomy 30:9-14

Deuteronomy is a covenant document, modeled after ancient covenants that were made between a king and his subjects. The contents of such documents laid out the requirements that the king expected of his subjects. But then at the end of such treaties were found a list of curses that would fall upon those who disobeyed the requirements (Deuteronomy 28:15-68), but also a list of blessings that would come upon those who obeyed (Deuteronomy 28:1-14; 30:1-10). Our text opens with a list of some of those blessings, in verse 9. God promises "good" (Hebrew) to all those who obey his commandments and his delight in all those who love him (cf. Deuteronomy 6:5).

At the center of Deuteronomy's law is the command to love God with all our heart and soul and might. At least eleven times, Deuteronomy sets forth that requirement for the covenant people of God, Israel, and of course our Lord repeats it for his church (Mark 12:30). The commandments in Deuteronomy, then, are intended to teach God's people how to love God, just as do the commandments of Jesus in the New Testament.

For many people in our congregations, however, it seems impossible to follow Jesus' requirements. Besides, they reason, we Christians are no longer under the law. Rather we are saved by grace alone through faith in Jesus Christ, who is the fulfillment of the law. And that is true. We are no longer under the law. We no longer have to work our way into favor with God. Through our participation by faith in the death and resurrection of Christ, we are counted righteous in the eyes of God.

Yet, our Lord Christ intends his commandments to be taken seriously (cf. Matthew 7:21). He expects us to obey them. And he does not think it is impossible to do so. Rather, Jesus' teaching is in accord with the words of Deuteronomy that we read in our text: "The word is very near you; it is in your mouth and in your heart, so that you can do it" (v. 14).

"God's love has been poured into our hearts through the Holy Spirit," writes Paul (Romans 5:5). "God has sent the Spirit of his Son into our hearts ..." (Galatians 4:6). "I will put my law on their hearts," Hebrews quotes from Jeremiah. God has poured out Christ's Spirit into our hearts, so that it is no longer we who live, but Christ who lives in us (Galatians 2:20), and by the power of his Holy Spirit, we are enabled to walk according to his commandments in newness of life.

Of course we cannot live the Christian life all by ourselves! Our sinful ways are always with us, and though we want to do good, we do just the opposite (cf. Romans 7:18-20). But God has not left us alone! Having sent his Son to redeem us from sin and death and to justify us in his sight, God through Jesus Christ now sends his Spirit to dwell in the hearts of all of those who trust him. And by that Spirit, you see, we can do far more abundantly than anything we ask or think. In the power of Christ's Spirit, we can do the good and obey our Lord's commandments and live a truly Christian life. By the Holy Spirit, "The word is very near you; it is in your mouth and in your heart, so that you can do it."

Proper 11

Amos 8:1-12

The lectionary often combines parts of two separate sections. The first three verses of this text represent the last of the four visions revealed to the prophet in 7:1-3, 4-6, 7-9, and 8:1-3. Verses 4-12 begin a long poem concerned with the "end" of Israel — the end of her injustice (vv. 4-8); the end of her worship (vv. 9-10); the end of hearing the Word of God (vv. 11-14); the end of her life (9:1-6).

Nevertheless, 8:4-8 helps explain why the "end" (v. 2) will come upon Israel. Her greed for gain and her injustice toward the poor have brought the sentence of death upon the nation. With the growth of commerce and urban culture during the reign of Jeroboam II (787/6-747/6 B.C.), many peasants lost their land and were at the mercy of food merchants.

The sabbath and festivals held each month at the time of the full moon were supposed to be days of rest from work and buying and selling. They were gracious gifts of God who ordains for us that we not only have work to do, but that we also have periods of rest and refreshment. But like us in our consumer culture, the merchants of Israel did not want to miss a chance to make some money. They chaffed at the days of rest when they could not sell, just as so many in our society would like to ignore Sunday's rest altogether and open the malls so we can go shopping.

The merchants of Israel were so greedy for gain, however, that when they were allowed to open for business, they cheated their innocent customers (v. 5). They made the "*ephah* small." That is, the standard forty liter vessel used to measure out grain was secretly reduced in size. The *shekel*, which weighed about 11.5 grams and which was put on a balance scale to determine how much silver was owed for the grain, was made heavier, thus costing the customer more money. Even the balance scales were "false," bent, so that they did not weigh accurately.

The poor could not afford such dishonesty and fell into debt to the merchants, while the merchants made enough extra cash to buy one of the poor as a slave for the meager price of a pair of sandals (v. 6). But the poor were desperate for food, and so sometimes they even scraped up the leavings of grain that had the chaff mixed in with it. And for that too the greedy merchants charged them! Anything to make a buck and never mind your neighbor!

The Lord of the Bible, however, is a just Lord, and there are few commandments that he gave to Israel that are emphasized more than the commandment to show justice toward all. "A full and just weight you shall have," God had said through Moses, "a full and just measure you shall have ... For all ... who act dishonestly are an abomination to the Lord" (Deuteronomy 25:15, 16). "You shall love your neighbor as yourself," Jesus taught us, quoting Israel's law (Mark 12:31; Leviticus 19:18). And part of the way that we love our neighbor is to treat him or her justly. Not to cheat. Not to take advantage. Not to count our own welfare greater than that of our neighbor. How far we sometimes fall short of that commandment of love!

The point of Amos, then, is that God sees these things. We have little thought of God when we buy or sell, don't we? We take little heed of the Lord when we indulge in our conspicuous consumption, and add goods to goods, comforts to comforts, and, set making more money as our goal. But God sees, God knows, and dear friends, God weeps. "Do not lay up for yourselves treasures on earth," Jesus taught us, "but lay up treasures for yourselves in heaven" (Matthew 6:19, 20). Seek first God's kingdom and his righteousness (Matthew 6:33).

Jesus spoke those words to us because God wants us to live, and as we learn from Amos, Israel in her greed and her neglect and injustice toward the poor, could not live. She forfeited her life. In 721 B.C., the ten northern tribes of Israel were carried into exile by the armies of Assyria, and they just disappeared from history. God did not forget Israel's greed and injustice, and those abominations cost Israel her life. Truly the teachings of the scriptures are a matter of life and death for us.

168

On this Sunday, as so many of us are heading out for vacations or returning from them, are these not things that we should ponder in our hearts and apply to our pocketbooks and our care for the poor? And should not we all perhaps repent and change the direction of our lives?

Lutheran Option: Genesis 18:1-10a

This story is simply an ancient and perhaps interesting — and even sometimes unbelievable — tale to a congregation unless they know its context. According to Genesis 12:1-3, God called Abraham and his family to leave their home in Mesopotamia and to journey to the land that God would show them. As part of that call, God promised Abraham that he would give him not only a land to call his own, but also many descendants. And most important of all, God promised that through Abraham's descendants, God would bring blessing on all the families of the earth. In Genesis 1-11, human beings live under the curse of broken community, of the loss of all good, and of death. But God sets out through Abraham to turn that curse into blessing.

In our story, therefore, Abraham and his wife and servants are journeying through the land of Canaan. They are both rather elderly — as 18:11 says, Sarah is past the age of childbearing. Nevertheless, the Lord promises Sarah that in the spring of the year, she will bear a son. And that birth will begin to fulfill God's promise to Abraham of many descendants.

We have three versions of this promise of a son in the Old Testament — in 15:1-6; 17:15-17; and here in chapter 18. This is probably the oldest version, but each writer has framed this important story in his own way. Certainly, however, this version has about it the most vivid and earthy character.

Mamre is located in the southern portion of Palestine, just north of Hebron. Abraham earlier built an altar at Mamre (13:18), and near the site is the field of Machpelah where the patriarchs and their wives later were all buried. But Mamre is southern and it is hot.

So Abraham is sitting quietly at the door of his tent at Mamre when suddenly, out of nowhere, three men stand in front of him.

169

Already a mysterious note is sounded in the story. Abraham is a model semite, however, who knows how to practice hospitality. As in our south, hospitality is a mark of a pious person. So Abraham runs to meet his visitors, begs them to stay for a meal, washes their feet, calls himself their servant, and tells Sarah quickly to prepare fine meal cakes. Then Abraham himself runs to select a calf, the most prized meat, and gives it to his servant, who hastens to prepare it. The note of haste, emphasizing hospitality, is prominent throughout the story. Abraham is doing everything to make his guests comfortable and welcome. He even waits on them while they eat by themselves.

In contrast to all such attentive hospitality, however, the guests ask a startling question. "Where is Sarah your wife?" (v. 9). That is a shocking query. What does this stranger know about Abraham's wife? Once again, a mysterious note is struck.

Finally, however, one of the three men is identified. "The Lord said" (v. 10). Abraham has been entertaining the Lord! God has suddenly appeared to him in human form! And the promise that God states is overwhelming. In the spring of the year, the Lord will return (v. 14) and Abraham's elderly wife will bear a son. The birth will not be a natural occurrence, but made possible only by God, because as verse 14 reads, nothing is too hard for the Lord.

It is rather unfortunate that the lectionary omits vv. 11-15, for they show the very human characteristics of Sarah, and indeed, of us all. Sarah has been eavesdropping behind the tent door flap on the conversation, and when she hears the promise, she laughs. She cannot believe it, just as Abraham himself does not at first believe it in the other versions of the story (cf. Genesis 15:2-3; 17:17). Sarah and Abraham, despite their pious hospitality, are no models of faith. They initially do not believe, and the son's name, Isaac, which means "laughter," enshrines that disbelief.

But nothing is too hard for the Lord, and his purpose is not defeated by unbelief. In the spring of the year, Isaac is born, in fulfillment of God's promise (Genesis 21:1-2). God's history of salvation is begun, and that history will finally come to its climax in the descendant of Abraham, Jesus Christ (cf. Matthew 1:1), the Savior of us all. God keeps his promises. Nothing is too hard for him. On those facts rests our faith.

170

Proper 12

Hosea 1:2-10

We are a whoring nation, are we not? And our harlotry is not only spiritual, so that we worship all sorts of deities besides the Lord. Our harlotry is also physical. Ours is a sex-saturated culture. Our magazines, our advertisements, the newspapers in our supermarkets all concentrate on sex and sexual attraction. Every romantic encounter on television automatically leads to bed. Pre-marital and extra-marital affairs are taken for granted. Our schools hand out condoms, our college students live on campuses rife with promiscuity. And often the center of our attention are those Hollywood and television "stars," who live together or have children together without a thought of getting married. We are absorbed with sex, even in our churches, and most of it is harlotrous and adulterous.

The result is that we are not too shocked when the Lord commands the prophet Hosea to "Go, take to yourself a wife of harlotry and have children of harlotry, for the land commits great harlotry by forsaking the Lord" (v. 2). But in our sex-saturated situation, perhaps we need to listen carefully to this story about the call of the prophet Hosea that comes to us from the eighth century B.C. northern kingdom of Israel.

Hosea is commanded by God to marry a "woman of harlotry." What does that mean? In Hosea's time, when Israel was shot through with the worship of the fertility gods or baals of Canaan, it means that the prophet was commanded by God to take as his wife a woman who had served, either once or frequently, as a so-called sacred prostitute at the worship site of Baal.

In baalistic religion, it was believed that various baal-gods "impregnated" the land, the mother goddess, with rain, causing it to bring forth produce. Similarly, the baal gods were understood to be the source of fertility in human beings. So by enacting the "marriage" of baal by means of sexual intercourse with male and female prostitutes at the cult site, worshipers thought to coerce the baal, by sympathetic magic, to bring forth fertility in both human beings and the land. In short, baal was believed to be the source of life, and worshiping him assured his devotees that they would have the good life.

The view was not too different from our modern belief that sex is the most important thing in our lives. If you don't have sex, our young people have been taught, you can't be a whole person. And if the sex life in a marriage isn't good, well then, you should abandon the marriage. A lot of people look to sexual intercourse for the source of the good life. But of course the real source of the good life — of abundant life — is God, isn't he? And that is the message that Hosea, by his sacrifice, is commanded to convey to his people.

Hosea suffers under the prophetic role given to him, as all the prophets suffer. After he marries the harlot Gomer, he watches the three children that she bears to him, playing in the courtyard. But only one of the children is said to be his. And the Lord commands him to give the children awful names: "Jezreel," (v. 4), the name of the place where the earlier king Jehu had fostered the worship of baal (2 Kings 10:29-31); "Not pitied" (v. 6), the sign that the Lord would no longer have any pity or mercy on his apostate people, but instead would send them into exile; and finally, "Not my people" (v. 9), the most ominous name of all. When God made a covenant with Israel at Mount Sinai, he had told them, "I will be your God and you will be my people" (Exodus 6:7; Leviticus 26:12, *et al*). Now God declares to Israel that they have destroyed his covenant bond with them, and they no longer belong to him. The covenant is abandoned, and God will no longer be with Israel as their God, for he now divorces them as his people.

Hosea's marriage and the naming of his children are prophetic "signs" to whoring Israel. Not only do they announce information, but they also begin God's action of judgment upon his whoring nation, a judgment that finally ends in the Assyrian exile of Israel in 721 B.C. and her disappearance from history. When God divorces his adulterous wife Israel, she is as good as dead.

Should we not wonder, then, what God's future is for our society, for a people that no longer knows faithfulness to God's commands about sex and marriage and who therefore no longer are faithful to our Lord? Running after the temptations, the thrills, the daring of unbridled sexuality, have we run away from our God? And therefore will God say to us, "You are not my people"? Have we lost his care for us, his pity and mercy, his forgiveness, and his abundant life? Indeed, have we lost the resurrection and its eternal life beyond the grave?

The editors who assembled the oracles of Hosea made a pattern of alternating Hosea's judgment oracles with passages concerning salvation. The lectionary therefore has attached verse 10 to our reading. But verses 10-11 are separate pronouncements, given much later in Hosea's ministry, and indeed, never fulfilled during Hosea's lifetime. The eighth-century kingdom of Israel goes into exile, and it dies. If the preacher uses verse 10, he or she should be aware of those facts of history. It is not until the birth of Jesus Christ that God's promises of salvation in Hosea's book are realized (cf. Matthew 2:15).

Lutheran Option: Genesis 18:20-32

This passage follows immediately on last Sunday's text, in which the three men appeared at the door of Abraham's tent in Mamre, and one of them, the Lord, promised the aged Abraham and Sarah a son. Now the question of the sin of Sodom is taken up in a marvelous conversation between the Lord and Abraham.

Abraham is not particularly interested in saving Sodom, that legendary symbol of sin that was located at the southern tip of the Dead Sea. (The site is now under water.) Nor does Abraham show any concern for his nephew Lot, who dwells in Sodom. Rather, the patriarch engages in a theological conversation with his God.

Abraham, like so many of us, is interested in the justice of God. God has revealed to Abraham that he is going to destroy Sodom (cf. vv. 17-19). But Abraham wants to know if righteousness counts more with God than does unrighteousness. If God finds fifty righteous in Sodom, will he spare the whole city on their account? Surely, the Judge of all the earth would not destroy them (v. 25)! Abraham has his own conception of what God should be like, and God patiently puts up with Abraham's questioning — perhaps with a smile on the divine face.

Abraham does have some awareness of his own boldness. "Behold, I have taken upon myself to speak to the Lord, I who am but dust and ashes," he says (v. 27). Such humility is fitting for a conversation with God. But that does not deter Abraham's boldness. If God finds forty-five, or forty, or thirty, or twenty, or just ten righteous persons in Sodom, will God spare the city for their sake? How much does righteousness weigh on the scales of God's justice?

But it is not justice that the Lord talks about in this passage. It is mercy. And for the sake of ten righteous persons in Sodom — or for the sake of one righteous man named Jesus Christ — God will not come to destroy us. Christ's righteousness on the cross and his victory at the resurrection atone for all our sins, and God counts us justified through faith in our Lord. An incredibly merciful, patient, loving God wills for us life instead of death.

If we should want a just measurement in the scales of God of all that we have done, not one of us would deserve life, because each one of us has sinned. And "the wages of sin is death, but the free gift" — totally undeserved, totally a gift of grace — "is eternal life in Jesus Christ our Lord" (Romans 6:23).

Proper 13

Hosea 11:1-11

Few passages in the Old Testament are more important than this one, because it sets forth central understandings of the nature of God and of his relation to Israel and to the course of world history.

When the Lord delivered that bunch of slaves from Egypt that later became the nucleus of his people in the thirteenth century B.C., he made them a people and adopted them as his son. Knowing that is absolutely necessary for understanding the Bible. Israel was God's adopted son. The Lord redeemed Israel, that is, he acknowledged Israel to be his family member whom he bought back out of slavery — that is the meaning of redemption (cf. Leviticus 25:47-55). And so from the time of the exodus onward, Israel is God's adopted son, and God is Israel's Father (cf. Exodus 4:22-23; Deuteronomy 32:6; Jeremiah 3:19; 31:20; Isaiah 1:2; 63:16; Malachi 1:6; 2:10).

What follows in this passage, therefore, are the tender scenes of God the Father caring for his adopted son. God taught infant Israel how to walk, holding out a finger for the child to grasp as he toddled along and stumbled and fell, and was lifted up again in his Father's arms (v. 3). Gently and compassionately God led Israel along the path of life by giving them his presence in the law (Deuteronomy 4:7) and granting them the guidance of the Word from prophets (cf. Amos 2:11) and priests.

Verse 4 of our text is often emended by changing one Hebrew vowel to read, "And I was to them as those who lift a baby to their check, and I bent down to feed him." Whether the emendation is accepted, or the verse is read as in the RSV, the tenderness and compassion of the Lord are clear.

But Israel has forgotten the tenderness and love of its Father and has run from God like a disobedient child. God has repeatedly called, and Israel has not listened (v. 2). Indeed, Israel is so set in its apostasy and worship of the fertility gods of baal, that it cannot return. "Their deeds do not permit them to return to their God, / For the spirit of harlotry is within them, and they know not the Lord" (Hosea 5:4).

They are slaves of their sin, Paul would say, captives to the habit of idolatry, just as we become habitually captive to our sin and forgetfulness of the One who made us. God calls us through his written and preached Word, and we do not listen, running out into the path of danger, with our Father pleading with us to stop.

The wages of sin is death, however (Romans 6:23), and disobedient Israel will receive that wage, just as every wanton one of us will be paid what we have earned. "Whatever a man sows, that he will also reap," writes Paul. "God is not mocked" (Galatians 6:7).

And yet — and yet — when God considers the death of his adopted people, he cries out in longing. "How can I give you up, O Ephraim! How can I hand you over, O Israel!" How can I make you like those cities of Admah and Zeboim that were destroyed along with Sodom and Gomorrah? (Deuteronomy 29:23).

The Bible tells us that God has no pleasure in the death of anyone. He just wants us to turn our lives around and to live (Ezekiel 18:32). And so God weeps over his disobedient child Israel, as our Lord wept over Jerusalem (Luke 13:34), and as he still weeps over us. And because he is pure and merciful love, he cannot give up us his children, any more than he could finally give up his adopted child Israel. At the end, writes Paul, "all Israel will be saved" (Romans 11:26). Beyond Israel's exile to Assyria, beyond its apparent destruction for its sin, there is a new and saved people of God that will know salvation.

The reason is plain. God is the Holy One (v. 9), that is, he is totally other than anything or anyone in all creation. His thoughts are not our thoughts, and his ways are not our ways (Isaiah 55:8-9), and his fatherly love for those whom he has made, for Israel and for us, is beyond all comprehension. So there is at the end of our passage, the glad picture of Israel saved and returned home — the dream of God for the future of his adopted son.

As for us, God's love is made manifest in the figure of a young man, hanging on a cross on a hill called Golgotha. There is God's declaration to us that he cannot give us up, despite all our wayward wandering from his fatherly directions, despite all our indifference toward the One who has taught us to walk, and constantly carried us in his arms, and continually bent down to feed us with his good. Instead of giving us up to the death that our sins so richly deserve, God gives up his only begotten Son, and you and I are offered the free gift of life in Jesus Christ.

It finally is a lesson in history, isn't it? — that the one fact that will triumph in this world is the love of God. For all the evil of nations, and despite all the wrong of the human race, God is sovereign over every form of evil. He was sovereign over Israel's sin, sovereign over Assyria that took her captive, sovereign over the power of Rome that nailed Jesus Christ to the cross. And he is yet sovereign over our lives, for which he wills only his eternal life and love. Who can refuse the Father of such amazing love?

Lutheran Option:
Ecclesiastes 1:2, 12-14; 2:18-23

These excerpts from Ecclesiastes could be a characterization of our society. The author of Ecclesiastes, who is called the Preacher, sets out to make an examination of the ways of Wisdom theology. And in that examination, he studies the work at which men and women toil. It is full of vexation, the author writes. A person strains to do a good job, takes his work home with him at night, worries about it on his bed, and gets up and does the same thing all over again the next day.

But what is the point of it all? the writer wants to know. To what does it lead? Nothing lasts. The contributions that you make are soon forgotten. The capital that you have accumulated may just be foolishly spent by your heirs. Two generations from now, even your relatives will no longer remember much about you.

> *As for man, his days are like grass;*
> *he flourishes like a flower of the field;*
> *for the wind passes over it, and it is gone,*
> *and its place knows it no more.* Psalm 103:15-16

177

All the pain, all the toil, all the anxiety and worry that we pour into our daily round finally are part of a transitory life that ends up in nothing — in vanity, nothingness, as the Preacher says. "Vanity, all is vanity."

To be sure, we all have to earn our daily bread and support our families and put a roof over their heads. And we all do try to do a good job at whatever labor we undertake. But the Preacher here in our text is asking the deeper question. What is the meaning of it all? What endures? What eternal significance does my little life or yours have in the course of history that just goes on and on and on?

Ecclesiastes' answer to that was simply to enjoy the life and work and family love that God has given us, and not to worry about the future. "There is nothing better for a man than that he should eat and drink, and find enjoyment in his toil" (v. 24). "Enjoy life with the wife whom you love, all the days of your vain life which (God) has given you under the sun ... Whatever your hands find to do, do it with your might; for there is no work or thought or knowledge or wisdom in Sheol (the place of the dead), to which you are going" (Ecclesiastes 9:9-10). To enjoy your brief span — that's the meaning of your life. As a young man said to me this summer, "I think the purpose of life is just to be happy."

The Apostle Paul knows differently, however, because he knows that Jesus Christ is risen. At the end of 1 Corinthians 15, which is Paul's great chapter on the resurrection, Paul tells us Christians, "Therefore, my beloved ... be steadfast, immovable, always abounding in the work of the Lord, knowing that in the Lord your labor is not in vain."

In God's service, you see, nothing is vanity and meaningless, because God uses that labor to further his purpose on earth. And finally, in God's love, our work is taken up into his eternal kingdom and perfected. And you and I end up not in the dark forgetfulness of the grave, but in the joyful company of God's everlasting family. If our lives are dedicated to the obedience, the service, the love of God, never are they in vain.

Proper 14

Isaiah 1:1, 10-20

In the popular piety that so dominates American religious life, there is the saying that "God hears every prayer." The first seventeen verses from these readings in Isaiah contradict that sentimental belief.

Once again the lectionary has combined two separate oracles in this reading. Verses 10-17 form what is known as a Torah instruction, that is, an instruction given by God as his Word. Verses 18-20, however, are a *rib*, a summons from God to go to court with him.

It is clear from the first passage that Judah in the time of Isaiah (745-701 B.C.) loved to go to worship. They literally "trampled" the courts of the temple, a picture that always reminds me of the crowds in our churches on Christmas and Easter. But the Judeans worshiped not only on high festival days, but on sabbaths and new moons at the first of each month and with a multitude of daily sacrifices to the Lord. And assuredly, as with us, their frequent worship gave them the sense that they were right with the Lord.

The astounding message from God is that he rejects it all, and his rejection is given in a series of ever more serious tones: "I cannot endure ..." (v. 13); "my soul hates ..." (v. 14); "I am weary of ..." (v. 14); "I will not listen." Judah's worship has become to God an unendurable, hateful, weary burden, and when the Judeans pray, God will no longer hear their prayers. God does not listen to every prayer! He shuts his ears against it!

For those who think they do God a favor when they go to church, that is a shocking message indeed. And for those of us who have a habit of prayer, it is incomprehensible. After all, we read over and over again in the Psalms the assertion, "On the day I called, thou didst answer me" (Psalm 138:3, *et al*). And does our Lord Jesus not tell us in his parable that we "ought always to pray and not lose heart" (Luke 18:1).

179

That which we overlook is another statement in the Psalms, however. "When the righteous cry for help, the Lord hears" (Psalm 34:17). The assumption is that the Lord hears prayer only when it is uttered by those who are just in his sight. And of course that is the problem with the Judeans in our text. They are not just. Verse 15 tells us that when the worshipers spread forth their hands in prayer, that which God sees on their hands is the blood of the innocent poor — the poor who have been denied justice in Judah's courts, the helpless who have been oppressed by those in power, the hungry who have not been fed, and the homeless who have not been sheltered.

That should give pause to all of us church-goers, who have come into the sanctuary to pray to God. Is there blood on our hands, indifference to justice in our hearts, callousness toward the helpless in our society? Do we minister to those in need, or like the priest and the Levite in the parable of the Good Samaritan, do we pass by on the other side? (Luke 10:29-32). Ours is a bloody, violent society these days — just read the morning headlines. And far too often ours is a heedless society, sometimes even indifferent toward the plight of our own children, whose lives are scarred by divorce or left helpless by poor schools or trained only by television programs, or even ended before they are ever born by our epidemic of abortion. Does God, then, hear our prayers? Do we have any just claim to come before him?

In both passages of our reading, God offers us a second chance. "Cease to do evil," he teaches, "learn to do good." "If you are willing and obedient, you shall eat the good of the land." God holds out to us the possibility of repentance and the assurance that we can be forgiven, if we will only turn to be "willing and obedient" to his Word.

That second chance, that turning, is offered to us through Jesus Christ. Let's face it. If you and I can only pray to God and have him hear our prayers when we are just, then not one of us has the remotest possibility of being acceptable to him. The only prayer we can have on our lips is: "God, be merciful to me, a sinner" (Luke 18:13). But that prayer, offered through the mediation and in the name of Jesus Christ, will be heard by our God, because

Christ has atoned for all of our shortcomings and sins and terribly human failings. And if we cling to Christ and his work on our behalf, God sees his Son's righteousness, and he hears and he answers.

More than that, however, God in his mercy grants us his Holy Spirit, to work in our hearts, so that we are gradually transformed and find that we are able to do the good and to cease doing evil. Christ's Spirit enables us to be willing and obedient servants of our God. Christ's Spirit can gradually make us new persons — new persons who go out and work in our society to establish justice and give help to the poor and bring an end to the bloodshed that stains us all. So the invitation is offered us through the words of Isaiah. We have only in faith to accept it.

Lutheran Option: Genesis 15:1-6

This passage forms the beginning of what scholars have called the Elohist's writings in the Old Testament, and it sets forth the first version of God's promise to Abraham of a son (cf. Genesis 17:15-16P; 18:10J). As such, it is rich in theological possibilities.

First, the promise of a son to be Abraham's heir is understood in the context of God's promise to Abraham to make him the father of a great nation and to bring blessing on all the families of the earth through his descendants (Genesis 12:1-3; see the exposition of Genesis 18, Proper 19). God here starts his centuries-long work of fulfilling his promise, that work that will finally result in the birth of Jesus Christ, "the son of Abraham" (Matthew 1:1). Through Christ, God will indeed bring his blessing upon all, as Paul asserts in Galatians 3:8-9.

The details of this story command our careful attention, however. When God speaks to Abram, his first words are "Fear not." That is often the first word that is spoken when God draws near to human beings, lest they be simply overwhelmed by the majesty and glory of the Lord. "Fear not, for behold, I bring you good tidings of great joy which shall be to all people" (Luke 2:10 KJV).

Having assured Abram, God promises him, "Your reward shall be very great," that is, your *posterity* shall be numerous. Abram, however, is very much like we are. He does not believe that promise! In fact, his response to the Word of God is almost blasphemous. God tells him, You will have many descendants, and Abram replies, "No, I won't." Obviously, it is not Abram's great faith that causes God to give him the promise, any more than it is our great faith that inspires God to give promises and good to us. God acts toward Abram and us simply out of his grace and mercy.

Abram believes that because he is an old man, the son of his slave-woman must be his heir. That is the law of the time, which finds its parallel in ancient Nuzi tablets of the fifteenth century B.C. Apparently it was a practice known throughout the ancient Near East.

But when God works to fulfill his promise, he takes little notice of human custom and law. Nor is he bound by what we call natural law and the seeming impossibility of an aged man and his wife having a son. Instead, God takes Abram outside in the night, and tells him to look at the stars and to number them if he can. "So shall your descendants be," God promises — as numerous as the stars of the heavens. Out of an aged couple will come a "great nation," in fulfillment of God's word (Genesis 12:2). The people Israel will exist on the earth only because God will bring them forth, and they will continue to exist on the earth, no matter how often or much they are persecuted, because they are God's people, created by him.

Having been told by God that his descendants will be as numerous as the stars in the heavens, the author of this passage records, "And (Abram) believed the Lord; and (the Lord) reckoned it to him as righteousness" (v. 6). Here we have in the Bible for the first time the doctrine of justification by faith. Abram is counted righteous in God's eyes because he believes God's promise.

We should note therefore the nature of faith. We often say that we are justified by faith alone, but what is faith? Here in our text we see clearly that faith is believing the promises of God and then acting accordingly. Faith is hearing what God promises and then clinging to those promises, believing that they will be fulfilled, no matter what happens. Faith is committing one's whole life to acting according to what God says he will do.

God has given us lots of promises in the Bible, and our Lord promised us many things, according to the New Testament. "I will not leave your desolate. I will come to you" (John 14:18). "He who believes in me, though he die, yet shall he live, and whoever lives and believes in me shall never die" (John 11:25). "Lo, I am with you always, to the close of the age" (Matthew 28:20). There are many examples. And our faith consists in believing those promises and acting as if we know they will be fulfilled, no matter what happens to us and no matter what the times bring upon us. God always keeps his promises. To that we can always say, "Amen."

Proper 15

Isaiah 5:1-7

This passage is famously known as Isaiah's "Song of the Vineyard." It begins with the prophet singing, in what we would describe as troubadour-fashion, a love song about his *dod*, his friend, the beloved. Everyone is interested in a love affair, of course, and so the song is intended to capture the interest of Isaiah's listeners.

The story that the song tells is simple. The beloved had a vineyard, upon which he lavished the most careful attention, clearing the ground, planting it with choice vines, building a watchtower to guard off wild animals, and even preparing a wine vat in anticipation of an abundant grape harvest. The beloved therefore expected the vineyard to yield choice grapes, *'anabim*. Instead its grapes were wild, *be'esim*, bitter and full of seeds. (The poem consistently gives contrasts by using Hebrew words that sound very much alike, but that have exactly the opposite meaning.)

Thus, as with a parable, the prophet's listeners are asked to make a decision. Was there anything more that the beloved could do for his vineyard? Obviously, the answer is no. The listeners are undoubtedly disgusted with such an unproductive crop. (Cf. the same device used by the prophet Nathan to arouse David's indignation in 2 Samuel 12:1-7.)

The result is that the beloved will stop caring for the vineyard, will break down its wall, let it be trampled and devoured by animals, and — most astounding of all — command the clouds to hold back their rain! With that sentence, the listeners are brought up short. Only God can command the rain, and the prophet's audience suddenly realizes that the love song has been about the Lord and his people Israel. The beloved is God in his constant and intimate care for his chosen folk, and Israel is his vineyard. That latter is a figure often used throughout the Bible (cf. Jeremiah 2:21; Psalm 80:8-16; Mark 12:1-11; John 15:1). And the final stanza of the song spells out that meaning. God looked for Israel to bring forth justice, mispat, and instead it produced bloodshed, mispah. He expected from Israel righteousness, *s'daqah*, and got the cry, *s'qah*, of the oppressed and poor instead.

It is not difficult to see ourselves in this song, for God has been our beloved, the one who loves us, for a very long time, has he not? Think of all the intimate care he has lavished upon us from our beginning. Job tells us that it was God who shaped us so carefully in our mother's wombs (Job 10:8-11), and then he brought us forth and gave us our breath of life, marking each one of us with our own individuality and fingerprints and DNA like no other. He was with us through all of our youth, though perhaps we did not know it, and now, says the Psalmist, he is acquainted with all of our ways, knowing when we sit down and when we rise (Psalm 139:2-3), surrounding us with his mercy as if with air. God even numbers the hairs of our heads, Jesus teaches (Matthew 10:30 and par.), and he knows our needs before we ever ask.

God loves us so much that, seeing our sins, our despair, our deaths that would separate us from him, he sent his beloved Son to take all of our miseries upon himself, dying that we might live with our God. And then God raised that Son and gave us the promise of eternal life with him in glory. All, all of that has been loved poured out upon this congregation assembled here this morning.

And what has God expected from us in response to his amazing love? Surely he can do no more for our abundant benefit than he has already done. So what should be our love in return for his love? Gratitude, dear vineyard of the Lord, gratitude. Thankfulness that issues in the will to praise and serve our Lord of love all our days. Gratitude that honors his loving lordship over our lives and tries each day to walk in the ways of goodness and justice and peace that he has set out before us. Loving us with all his mighty heart, God expects from us love and obedience to him with all our hearts and might, in every thing we do. That is the "reasonable service" of anyone who loves the Lord (cf. Romans 12:1-3).

186

Lutheran Option: Jeremiah 23:23-29

This is a dangerous passage for a minister to preach, because it is dealing with false prophecy. It comes at the end of the collection of Jeremiah's oracles on the false prophets (Jeremiah 23:9-32), and it deals with those prophets who have been preaching "peace, peace" to the people of Judah, when the people actually have no peace with God (cf. 6:14; 8:11).

Ignoring the people's sin and the coming judgment of God upon it, the false prophets are like our "therapeutic preachers" of today. Their aim is to make their audiences feel good about themselves, assuring the people that all is well, and that God accepts and loves them just the way they are, with no necessity for the listeners to change their ways.

But, says Jeremiah, the false prophets are saying, "Thus says the Lord," when the Lord has not sent them (Jeremiah 23:31-32). They have not "stood in the council of the Lord to perceive and to hear his word" (23:18). Jeremiah is referring to God's heavenly council (cf. 1 Kings 22:13-28 for the scene). But in our terms, the false prophets have not had that intimate, daily communion with God from which issues true prophetic speech. In fact, the false prophets even steal oracles from one another (Jeremiah 23:30), a practice not unknown in our day among some clergy. Occasionally, whole sermons are clipped out of seminary library books, to be used by preachers. And I personally have heard of preachers who dishonestly use one of my published sermons as their own. We have our own false prophets in our society.

Certainly our society is full of religious messengers these days, those who claim to speak for God, or those who maintain that they have a new revelation from God. Televangelists, authors of religious books, New Age gurus of every sort, feminist re-imaginers, self-appointed "doctors" of theology, media reports — on every hand, we are barraged with so-called spiritual messages, and it becomes confusing sometimes to know how to separate the true Word of God from the utterances of our present-day false prophets. Those in New Testament times had the same difficulty.

Beloved, do not believe every spirit, but test the spirits
to see if they are of God; for many false prophets have
gone out into the world.   1 John 4:1

And the Book of Deuteronomy found it necessary to give two tests of true prophecy (Deuteronomy 13:1-3; 18:21-22), tests which are still a good measure for us.

First, says Deuteronomy, if a prophet tells you to go after and serve other gods whom you have not known, that is a false prophet and "you shall not listen to the words of that prophet" (Deuteronomy 13:2-3). In short, those of us who follow Jesus Christ know there is one God, the Father of our Lord. He is the God to whose word we cling in faith and obedience. Therefore, when you hear someone tell you that he is speaking in the name of the Lord, ask yourself, "Do that person's words accord with the true revelation of God that we have in Jesus Christ? Do they accord with what the universal church everywhere has always believed?"

Second, Deuteronomy says that if a prophet's words come to pass, they are truly the Word of the Lord. Indeed, that is why the oracles of the prophets that we have in the Old Testament have been preserved — because their words came to pass.

Lying behind that is an understanding of the Word of God. As our text for the day says, in Jeremiah 23:29, the Word of the Lord is like fire, or like a hammer that breaks rock in pieces. The Word of the Lord is powerful; it brings about results. So when you hear someone preaching a message from God these days, ask yourself, "Is this the Word of the same God who overcame sin at the cross of Jesus Christ and who conquered death on Easter morn? Is this the Word of God that created a people and a church and guided them and comforted them, judged them and saved them through all the ages? Or is this some alien word of a false prophet that has no power?" The Word of God does that of which it speaks, and if you line up some modern word of some preacher against the revelation of God in Jesus Christ, given us in the scriptures, you will know if the preacher is a false messenger of God or a true one.

Proper 16

Jeremiah 1:4-10

You and I and all persons in our day are not prophets in the Old Testament sense of the word. They were given new words from God, which illumined where and how and why God was at work in Israel's life. But for us, the Word of God has now been fully revealed in the person of Jesus Christ. In his Son, God sums up and incarnates the whole of Old Testament prophecy. While we ministers are called to speak the Word of God, we therefore have no new word to proclaim, but rather we are called to proclaim Jesus Christ and to spell out what he means for life in our past, present, and future. So our speaking of the Word of God is secondary and dependent on the prior biblical word.

The Old Testament prophets received God's word in an ecstatic state, sometimes through dreams or visions, most often in direct speech from God. And we do not share that almost unexplainable, ecstatic, direct revelation anymore. Indeed, we are apt to put any one who claims it in a mental hospital. God revealed himself to his prophets of old in a unique manner.

Further, the history into which the prophets released God's word is not our history. The ninth through the fifth centuries B.C. in Israel's life were vastly different from our times, and we cannot automatically transfer the prophets' words to apply to our situations.

Nevertheless, in our text, when God calls the youthful Jeremiah in 626 B.C. to be a prophet to the nations, the Lord reveals some of the characteristics of his divine nature, and it is that revelation that is important for us.

God comes to the young man Jeremiah in the most intimate fashion in this call. Jeremiah is not overwhelmed by the glory of God, as Ezekiel was (Ezekiel chs. 1-3) nor is he led to cry out over his sins when he beholds God's moral purity, as did Isaiah (Isaiah 6:1-5). Rather, God assures the youth that he has loved (= "known")

Jeremiah and planned for him to be a prophet even before Jeremiah was born. God is "with" Jeremiah. He touches the young man, and assures him that he will always deliver him.

You and I have no lesser assurance. All of us have been created in our mothers' wombs, the scriptures tell us (cf. Psalm 139:15-16), and God has a plan for each of our lives (cf. Philippians 1:6). We are not accidents of nature or even products of solely human love. Rather, we are the planned creations of the living God, who promises therefore to be with us to the end of history (Matthew 28:20).

Jeremiah, however, is a very unwilling servant of God, as we often are unwilling. He is called to proclaim God's words not just to Israel, but to the nations — an overwhelming task, for which he has neither talent nor experience. God, throughout the scriptures, seems to call the most unlikely persons to serve his purpose. As Paul writes, "God chose what is foolish in the world to shame the wise, God chose what is weak in the world to shame the strong" (1 Corinthians 1:27). And yes, God calls even us insignificant souls to do his work, in order that all may see that the work comes solely from God and not from our talents or abilities (cf. 2 Corinthians 12:7-9).

God equips us unlikely servants, however, as he equipped Jeremiah, and all of our inadequacies for our God-given tasks are overcome by God's all-sufficiency. To Jeremiah's "I do not know," God replies, "I knew you" (vv. 6, 5). To Jeremiah's "I am only a youth," God answers, "I am with you." "My grace is sufficient for you," the Lord told the Apostle Paul (2 Corinthians 12:9). And God's grace is always sufficient for us.

God is working out a plan of salvation in human history, a plan that he has laid very carefully from the beginning of human disobedience. We read that even before Jeremiah was formed in the womb, God knew how he wanted to use Jeremiah in his service, and how Jeremiah would fit into God's working toward his goal. And that is why Jeremiah was created, not simply to live out his days, not just to be his own person, but to be God's person, set apart (= "consecrated") for God's purpose. And that was the meaning of Jeremiah's life, as it is always the meaning of ours.

If any sense characterizes modern life these days, it is a sense of meaninglessness, of not knowing why we are here or what we are supposed to be and do. But as a church catechism puts it, we are born "to glorify God and to enjoy him forever" — in all we do to honor God, and in every moment to enjoy his company. And so our hearts are always restless until we rest in God, aren't they?

But who is this God we are called to serve? He is the Lord over all the earth. Jeremiah is called to preach the Word of God that will pluck up nations and break them down, that will build and plant others. God rules over the affairs of the world, despite all of our beliefs or evidence to the contrary. And you and I are called to serve a God who is Lord of all. It is an incredibly honorable task. Think of it! You and I, humble little souls that we are, are nevertheless called to be servants in the purpose of the King of the Universe! We are called to be instruments whom God uses to bring in his kingdom on earth. Surely there is no higher purpose for our living!

Lutheran Option: Isaiah 58:9b-14

This passage forms the last two stanzas (vv. 9b-12, 13-14) of the long poem that begins in Isaiah 58:1. Third Isaiah (chs. 56-66) is very much a situational book that reflects the conflict between the ruling Zadokite priests and the Levitical priests who have been ousted from their leadership of worship by the Zadokites, returned from Babylonian exile. Thus verse 9 of our text refers to the scorn and persecution that the Zadokites have inflicted upon the Levites.

If we generalize the text, however, it concerns both ethics and worship. The post-exilic Israelites are promised that if they minister to the hungry and afflicted in their society, then the Lord will be with them. And the Lord's presence is described in terms of "light" (cf. v. 8), as often throughout Third Isaiah (cf. 60:1, 19-20). By God's "light," the people will be guided in the proper way (v. 11). And by God's presence, the people will be given new vitality (= their bones made strong, v. 11). God is like a spring of living water (cf. Jeremiah 2:13; John 4:14) that gives life to withering plants, and so invigorated by the presence of the Lord, the people will be enabled to rebuild ruined Jerusalem (v. 12).

Another condition of God's presence with them is given in the last strophe (vv. 13-14). If the people keep the sabbath rest and honor it by not simply pursuing their own ways, then God will not only be with them, but they will "delight" in God's company, in exaltation and abundance.

We must be clear about the meaning of the sabbath in the Old Testament, however. Just as God rested on the seventh day of creation (Genesis 2:2-3), the sabbath is set apart ("hallowed") for Israel as a day of rest. We often misinterpret the meaning of the sabbath, and think that it is a command (Exodus 20:8-11) to go to church. Thus, we turn what was meant by God to be a gift of grace into a legalistic duty. But the Old Testament is clear; the sabbath is set apart as a day when we and all of our household may rest. (Exodus 20 even includes animals in the rest.)

We are very busy modern creatures, working hard at our jobs, running hither, to and fro, on errands of importance, fretting and worrying over the dozens of obligations that press in upon us. But on one day of the week, God says to us, "Take a break. Rest. Relax."

That is sheer grace on God's part. We haven't earned any rest. But nevertheless, a merciful God provides an opportunity for us to cease from work. And his command to us is that we extend that privilege to everyone around us.

In the Christian Church, we have equated the sabbath with Sunday, of course, but the two are not the same. Every Sunday is a worship-celebration of the resurrection of Jesus Christ and we go to church to participate in that celebration. But the sabbath, affirmed by our Lord, was made for man, not man for the sabbath (Mark 2:27), and it is set apart by God to give his creatures rest.

Our text implies that we should be grateful for such mercy, not concentrating on ourselves, but delighting in God's gift. For the sabbath is also a way of realizing God's constant care over us.

Proper 17

Jeremiah 2:4-13

This passage forms some of the earliest preaching of Jeremiah after his call in 626 B.C. and before the reform instituted by King Josiah of Judah in 621 B.C. The oracle is framed in terms of a court case, in which the Lord is the plaintiff, Judah is the accused, and the heavens serve as the jury (v. 12).

The main theme of the passage is given in verse 5. Judah "went after worthlessness," namely the fertility gods of Baal, "and became worthless." The poem is then divided into four stanzas (vv. 5-6, 7-8, 9-11, 12-13), and each of the last three stanzas or strophes ends with the same thought. In the second stanza, the false prophets "went after things that do not profit" (v. 8), that is, that are worthless. The end of the third stanza reads, "my people changed their glory," that is, their God, "for that which does not profit" (v. 11). And at the end of the fourth stanza, the people have hewed out for themselves cisterns "that can hold no water" (v. 13), in other words, cisterns that are worthless. The whole oracle, therefore, is concerned with the empty, useless worship and service of gods that are worthless.

The poem is a model of rhetorical skill, and when a theme is made so prominent in a poem, that should be the subject of the sermon on it. The preacher therefore will want to speak of our pursuit of worthless gods and goddesses — not a difficult subject in our time.

As the Lord presents his case against Judah in this text, the people's forgetfulness and ingratitude for God's saving deeds toward them in the past are highlighted. The people have not sought the gracious God who delivered them from bondage in Egypt and led them for forty years through the terrors of the wilderness (v. 6). When the Lord brought them into the promised land, flowing with milk and honey, where Judah inherited abundant water supplies and grain and vines, fig trees and pomegranates, where olives grew on the trees, and from whose hills they could dig copper (Deuteronomy 8:7-10), the covenant people enjoyed all those gifts, but thanked the baals for them instead (cf. Hosea 2:8). Even the priests and prophets, who were supposed to teach the people the traditions about God's saving acts, turned to the worship of the fertility gods. And the rulers acquiesced in such idolatry (Jeremiah 2:7-8).

That a nation should change its gods, however, is unheard of among other nations, especially when the new gods are without benefit for the people (vv. 10-11). Judah's "glory" was the Lord who constantly worked mighty deeds in her life. But Judah exchanged that glory for worthless deities.

All of that presents pictures aptly suited to our society. This nation of ours, founded so largely by Protestants and Catholics, always has pointed in the past to God as the source of its blessings. And certainly the church can tell the long history of God's deeds on its behalf, beginning with the death and resurrection of Christ, that freed us from bondage to sin and death. Through almost 2,000 years of church history, God has guided and sustained his church, raising up leaders in every generation, renewing its life when the church was failing, pouring out his forgiveness and love in countless benefits for individuals and congregations.

But now, what do we find? Very few in any congregation know the story of God's saving deeds preserved for us in the scriptures. Very few can name the Ten Commandments or state the basic doctrines of the Christian Church. Instead, many have made up their own right and wrong, their own beliefs, and yes, their own gods. And syncretism, re-imagining, idolatry, indifference, hedonism, run rampant through a people that is supposed to be the body of Christ.

The Lord calls upon the jury in our text, namely upon the heavens, to be utterly shocked at the condition to which Judah has sunk. Then the sentence is announced in the court case. "Be utterly desolate," God says to the heavens, that is, "dry up the rain." Judah thinks Baal is in charge of the rain that gives the good life of fertility, but the Lord is really in charge. And as the judgment on his faithless people, God takes back his gifts of life (v. 12). "The wages

194

of sin is death" in the Old Testament as well as the New (Romans 6:23).

The sin of the people of Judah is then summed up in the final verse. God is the only fountain of "living waters," the free-flowing stream of grace that can give life to a people. As Jesus tells the Samaritan woman in John 4:14, "Whoever drinks of the water that I shall give him will never thirst; the water that I shall give him will become in him a spring of water welling up to eternal life." From the one God, the Father of our Lord Jesus Christ, comes all life and good and eternity. Let us not exchange that everlasting fountain for worthless deities, broken cisterns in the desert, who have no measure of life-giving grace with which to provide us.

Lutheran Option: Proverbs 25:6-7

This Wisdom saying fits well with the Gospel reading from Luke 14:7-11, and indeed, may have been in Jesus' mind when he told the Lukan parable. If you are invited to the banquet of a king, do not try to sit or stand close to his royal person in order to make yourself noticed and important. Someone a lot more important than you may also be there, and you will be asked to move to a lower station to make room for the other. You will therefore suffer humiliation and be shown up for the self-serving individual that you are.

In the Proverbs text, verses 2-8 form a collection of Wisdom teachings concerned with life in a royal court, and they are meant to give instruction about how to conduct oneself in such a setting. Proverbs, in the Old Testament, are collections gleaned from observation of natural and human life that give instructions about how things and persons normally behave and about how to live a wise and ordered life in relation to them.

By using this Wisdom saying in his teaching, however, Jesus gives it an entirely different purpose. Now it becomes a parable about the Kingdom of God, and it deals with human pride. We see an example of such pride in the story of the disciples James and John who ask to sit at the right hand of Jesus when he comes into his glory in the kingdom (Mark 10:35-37).

The Christian life is not concerned with self-exaltation and self-importance, however. Indeed, Christian discipleship involves letting our selves be crucified — in Jesus' words, taking up our cross and following him to Golgotha. Discipleship involves giving up our own desires, our own will, our own plans and directions, and letting God in Christ replace them with his will and guidance and goals instead. As Paul writes, "It is no longer I who live, but Christ who lives in me" (Galatians 2:20). Christ has taken over Paul's life, and the Lord wishes to take over our lives as well. If we exalt ourselves and are concerned only with our own well-being, we shut out God. But if we humble ourselves and let God rule our days, he can use us in his good purpose.

Proper 18

Jeremiah 18:1-11

Have you ever seen a potter at work at his wheel? If you have, you know that fashioning pottery can be a very strenuous exercise. Potters don't "make a pot." They "throw a pot." The clay is thrown upon the wheel, pounded, whirled, shaped by the artisan's hands and fingers, until it takes the form that the potter wishes for it.

So it is with Israel, according to our text for the morning, and so it is with us. God the Potter is fashioning us into the people that he wants us to be. And sometimes it seems as if he works very strenuously with us, turning us about from some direction we have taken, pounding us with adversity, shaping us by the ups and downs of our daily life until we become the people he wants us to be. But it is all for the purpose of making us into cups that can contain a drink of cold water or into earthen vessels that can hold the treasures of his gospel.

The divine Potter works not only with individuals, however, but also with whole nations, shaping and forming or shattering and discarding. Our text is quite clear about God's sovereignty over all nations, and we must remember that our lives are finally subject not to international politics or multinational corporations or military planning, but to the will of the Lord who rules all of human history.

This narrative in the prophecies of Jeremiah comes from the Deuteronomic strand of material found so copiously in the prophet's book. It records an action of the prophet and the Word of God that came to Jeremiah in the early years of his ministry, after the failure of the Deuteronomic reform in 621 B.C. and before the death of the good king Josiah in 609 B.C. Josiah had tried to reform his apostate nation, banning all Canaanite practices and the worship of the pagan Canaanite gods. But as verse 12 indicates, the people of Judah had refused to change their idolatrous and unjust practices, despite the fact that they had renewed their covenant with the Lord on the basis of the laws of Deuteronomy (2 Chronicles 34-35).

Yet the Lord is incredibly merciful, wanting always to forgive and to restore, if his people will amend their ways and dedicate their hearts anew to God. That mercy is spelled out for Jeremiah and through him, for us, in this analogy to a potter's work. As an artisan works with a lump of clay, occasionally the clay seems to have a mind of its own, taking a shape that the potter never intended. But that does not mean that the potter simply throws away the clay and chooses another lump. No. The potter starts over with the same lump, and reworks it until it has the desired form.

The message is clear for Judah. She is not a covenant people whose ways are pleasing to her Lord. But God will not discard her and forget his covenant with her. Instead he will reform, rework, reshape her life, if she will let him do so.

None of us is beyond God's reforming and renewal of us. Our sinful past need not determine our future. Our divine Potter can mercifully forget our past. He can "remove our transgressions from us" "as far as the east is from the west" (Psalm 103:12). He can make us anew. The old can be done away. We can become God's new creations through Jesus Christ (2 Corinthians 5:17). But we must be willing to let God work that transformation in our sinful lives. We must respond to his mercy, accept his invitation to become new, commit ourselves into his hands to be shaped and molded to his will.

Judah was not willing to allow God that sovereignty. She was the vessel that strived with her Maker, the clay that resisted the Potter (Isaiah 45:9). And so she was destroyed by the armies of Babylonia and sent into exile. Yet, even then, God would not throw her away forever. And afterwards he promised her a future and a hope (Jeremiah 29:10-11).

Should we resist such persistent love that will not discard us as useless? God wants to make of us beautiful earthen vessels into which he can pour his joy and love and which he can use for his purpose. There really is no higher calling that we could have on this earth.

Lutheran Option: Deuteronomy 30:15-20

Israel is portrayed as camped in Moab on the eastern side of the Jordan, in the Book of Deuteronomy, looking over into the land that God promised from the first to her forbears. But before she crosses over into the land, Moses delivers three farewell addresses to the people. Those words are contained in the first 26 chapters of the book. In chapters 27-30, then, the Sinai covenant with the Lord is renewed, and this passage forms the closing instruction of that covenant.

Israel's entrance into the land of Canaan will form for her, in Deuteronomy's theology, a time of testing. Will she remain faithful to the Lord who has delivered her from slavery in Egypt, and who has guided her through the terrors of the wilderness, giving her manna to eat and water from the rock? Or will she go after the fertility gods of the Canaanites and seek her good and her life from them?

Israel stands at midpoint in her journey. Her redemption out of slavery lies in the past. Her entrance into the good life of rest and salvation in the promised land lies ahead. And in that situation, Israel's journey is very much like ours in our pilgrimage with God. We too are at the midpoint between our redemption out of slavery to sin and death by the cross of Christ and our final salvation in the Kingdom of God. The question of Deuteronomy is therefore very much a question for us also. Will we be faithful to the God who redeemed us and who has guided us through the wildernesses of our lives? Or will we run after other gods and things and look to them for our good and salvation? We too face the test of our faith, the test that can give us life or death, blessing or curse.

Our Lord Jesus set that test very clearly before us in the Sermon on the Mount. "Enter by the narrow gate," he taught, "for the gate is wide and the way is easy that leads to destruction, and those who enter by it are many. For the gate is narrow and the way is hard, that leads to life, and those who find it are few" (Matthew 7:13-14). Life or death, blessing or curse. We still face that choice.

Deuteronomy is very clear as to what we are to do in order to choose life. Four verbal phrases in our text characterize that choice:

"obey the commandments," "loving the Lord," "walking in his ways," "keeping his commandments" (v. 16). At the center of Deuteronomy's law is the command to love the Lord with all our heart and soul and might (Deuteronomy 6:5), and we have that love, says Deuteronomy, when we obey the Lord's commandments and walk according to his will, given us in the scriptures. Jesus said the same thing. "If you love me, you will keep my commandments" (John 14:15).

But that is not a legalistic command in either Old Testament or New. It points to our obedience out of a heart full of gratitude for all that the Lord has done for us. As 1 John would say, "We love because he first loved us" (1 John 4:19). We respond in obedience to God's love by walking in the way of his guidance in his commandments, given us in the scriptures. And that love and that obedience, proclaim both Testaments, form the way to life and not death, to blessing and not curse. If we desire life, abundant life, pressed down and running over, that comes from the Lord who redeemed us and whom we now love with all our hearts.

Proper 19

Jeremiah 4:11-12, 22-28

"Now it is I who speak in judgment upon them" (v. 12). Ours is a society that does not accept that as the Word of God. Many people do not believe that God judges anyone. Rather, the Lord is a forgiving God, a kindly deity who overlooks all wrong. As in the Gospel lesson for the morning, the Lord searches for the one lost sheep and returns it gently to the fold, or he hunts for the one lost coin until he finds it. God accepts the lost as they are, we think, overlooking Jesus' teaching about repentance and transformation of life.

The reason we discard all notions of God's judgment, moreover, is because we have lost all sense of right and wrong. No one is held responsible for his or her acts anymore. If they do evil, it is just because they are victims of society's structures, or their parents didn't raise them right, or they were under the influence of drugs or other outside forces. Right and wrong have become relative terms, subject to individual circumstances. And responsibility to a sovereign Lord is no longer considered to be applicable. If there is no responsibility, there is no sin, however, and therefore there is no occasion for God's judgment.

The prophets of Israel and our Lord Jesus knew differently. All persons, they knew, were responsible to the God who had made them, and Israel in particular had entered into a covenant with the Lord in which she promised to trust and obey him, just as all Christians renew that covenant every time they sit at the Lord's table. When Israel or we fail in our covenant with God, therefore, we are responsible to him for our thoughts and actions, and when we do not repent and turn our lives around to walk in God's ways, he is justified in his judgment of us.

Our text comes from the early days of Jeremiah's ministry, before 609 B.C., when Judah refused to repent. Instead, she gave

201

her allegiance to the pagan fertility gods of the Baal religion; she denied justice to the poor and oppressed; her prophets and priests were corrupt, seeking only wealth and approval for themselves; her covenant obligations were totally forgotten — all failings that could be duplicated in our present society. Indeed, Jeremiah tells us in the following chapter 5 that he searched Jerusalem for one righteous person and found none, among either the poor or the rich. And in his famous temple sermon in chapter 7, the prophet proclaims that the people thought their worship in the temple of the Lord was simply a hiding place ("a den of robbers") from the consequences of their sin (Jeremiah 7:8-11).

Our passage therefore sets forth two scenarios of God's judgment upon his faithless people. First, God's punishment is likened to the hot desert sirocco that blew into Judah to wither and dry up everything before it. Secondly, however, Jeremiah envisions an absolute judgment in which God reverses his very act of creation of the world.

Verses 23-28 deliberately parallel Genesis 1 and 2. The prophet sees the universe returned to chaos and void, as it was before God's creation of it (Genesis 1:2). The light is taken away (Genesis 1:3), the mountains and hills quake in the chaotic waters (cf. Psalm 46:2-3) and fall, birds and beasts and human beings disappear, and there is nothing left but the bare desert that can support no life (Genesis 2:4-5). In short, God takes back his creation. He is "sorry that he made man on the earth" (Genesis 6:6). And so earth and humankind are destroyed in God's last apocalyptic judgment.

Our fear is that a nuclear attack will destroy the universe. Perhaps our proper fear is that God, in his judgment on us, will bring it to an end. God made the world in the beginning. He determines its destiny. And he is quite capable of doing away with that which he has made. As Karl Barth once wrote, "The miracle is not that there is a God. The miracle is that there is a world" — that God decided to create us in the first place and that he has put up with us and our evil as long as he has.

The call for our repentance in the Gospel lesson, with its promise of God's mercy, is therefore our only hope of salvation.

Lutheran Option: Exodus 32:7-14

This text forms a vivid account of our sin. Israel is at Mount Sinai. She has entered into covenant with her God (Exodus 24:1-11), and she has twice vowed, "All that the Lord has spoken we will do" (Exodus 19:8; 24:3). In short, she has promised that her life will be ordered according to the Ten Commandments (Exodus 20:1-17), that she will have no other God besides the Lord. But at the very mount of covenant, almost immediately after she has pledged her heart and her life to her God, she falls into sin and makes for herself a golden calf to worship.

Is that not the way with us also? That we partake of the Lord's Supper, in which we vow our sole trust and obedience to our Lord Jesus, and then before we even get out of the church, we violate his commandments — gossiping about a neighbor, looking down on some poor soul, seeking our own status, turning our hearts and thoughts to the day's occupations with no thought of our God. Indeed, we leave the church, and it becomes business as usual, the daily preoccupation of seeking our own security and importance. And so we think to save our lives and, in Jesus' words, we will lose them instead.

The Israelites in our text have some remnant of piety. They know that it is the Lord who redeemed them from slavery. They know that forever after, the one true God is to be identified by that act. "I am the Lord your God, who brought you out of the land of Egypt, out of the house of bondage" (Exodus 20:1), just as we know that it is the God and Father of our Lord Jesus Christ who redeemed us from our bondage to sin and death. And so the Israelites have to claim that the idol they have made is the one who redeemed them (v. 8). And so often we attribute to Christianity some idol we have constructed for ourselves.

But there is one God alone who redeemed Israel and us from our slavery. And when we attribute that act to other gods, we violate our covenant with the Lord. God therefore is about to destroy Israel at the foot of Mount Sinai, just as he may destroy us.

Moses therefore fulfills the prophetic function of interceding for his sinful people, reminding God of his promise to Abraham,

Isaac, and Jacob. Moses is the intercessor who turns aside God's judgment on his sinful people.

We can thank a merciful God that we too have a mediator, who interceded for us on the cross. "Father, forgive them for they know not what they do" (Luke 23:34). By his pleading for us, and by his sinless death, Jesus Christ turned aside the judgment of God on us that we, like faithless Israel, so richly deserve. And indeed, writes Paul, the risen and ascended Christ continues to intercede on our behalf before the Father (Romans 8:34). But it is all for the sake of enabling us to repent and to return in trust and obedience to the one true God, so that we walk in newness of life and in the joy and peace and salvation with the Father that he so much desires for us.

Proper 20

Jeremiah 8:18 — 9:1

This moving elegy is the passage from which the Negro spiritual, "There is a balm in Gilead," is taken, although that spiritual turns the negative questioning of verse 22 into a positive assurance of healing. But in Jeremiah's time, there is no healing for sinful Judah.

The poem follows immediately on those judgment pronouncements in Jeremiah that deal with the mysterious, transcendent "Foe from the North," 8:14-17 forming the last of those oracles. (For the others, see 4:5-8, 13-18, 29-31; 5:15-17; 6:1-8, 22-26.) In a prophetic vision, the prophet sees the imminent destruction of his beloved people at the hand of God, and he weeps, as Jesus wept over Jerusalem (Luke 19:41-44).

Jeremiah hears in his ears his people crying out in alarm (v. 19; cf. a similar hearing in 4:19-21). And he portrays the future desperate dialogue that the people will have with God. They will question why the God who dwells in the Holy of Holies on Mount Zion is attacking them, and God will reply that Judah has provoked him with their idols. The people will mourn that the summer — the season of military adventure — has brought them no ally's salvation (v. 20). And they will be wounded (v. 21). No healing balm from Gilead, famous for its medicinal cures, will be available. Sinful Judah will not be restored to health, but instead will be destroyed by the Babylonians and her people carried into exile, first in 597 B.C. and then decisively in 587 B.C. Jeremiah sees and hears it all in a vision of the future, and he is sick at heart (v. 18) and weeps day and night (9:1) over his people's coming ruin.

That which is so noteworthy in this passage is not the vision of Judah's future destruction; many passages announce that imminent fate. Rather, the prominent feature is Jeremiah's identification with his sinful people. When we witness the downfall of a wrongdoer, we are all too apt to gloat over his just punishment. Or when we know someone in the church who is nevertheless not acting in a Christian manner, we separate ourselves from her and consider ourselves righteous compared to her unrighteousness. Even some preachers fall victim to such pharisaism, considering themselves on God's side and the sinful and stubborn people on the other. Not Jeremiah, and not any of the prophets of the Old Testament. They know themselves to be bound up in the bundle of life with their sinful folk, and they share the misery of that faithless people. Indeed, they suffer first in their own lives the judgment that is coming upon Israel. And so Jeremiah's heart is broken before Judah's is wounded.

The further fact is that Jeremiah's grief is not only his, but also God's. God has no pleasure in the death of anyone (Ezekiel 18:32). When he sees that "the imagination of the thoughts of (our) hearts" are "only evil continually," his reaction is not wrath, but grief (Genesis 6:6). And when Jesus foresees the future destruction of Jerusalem, he mourns, "O Jerusalem, Jerusalem ... How oft would I ... and ye would not" (Luke 13:34). There therefore follows our text in Jeremiah, two verses in which God, in his weariness with his sinful people, mourns their evil ways (Jeremiah 9:2-3). Not only Jeremiah's heart is stricken, but also God's — that great heart of mercy that wants so very much only our good. And Jeremiah's tears are the tears of the God who loves us beyond all our imagining.

Lutheran Option: Amos 8:4-7

It has often been said that commercialism has become the dominant note in American society. Our primary goal in life has become the accumulation of wealth, in order that we may buy more things that will give us comfort and status. Most families now are two-worker families, because a high standard of living cannot be maintained without two paychecks. And without that standard we are not considered successful or important. The "beautiful people" are those who capture our interest, because they can afford to live in luxury — witness the television program about the lives of the rich and famous. We admire those who have money, and every year we read, sometimes with envy, the list of the wealthiest Americans. Making money is the national goal, our bottom line for life.

Human beings change very little over the centuries, and that was the goal of the merchants in Amos' eighth century B.C. Israelite society also. Indeed, they were impatient with anything that prevented them from making a shekel. Especially were they impatient and vexed over Israel's worship days when commerce was not allowed.

Most of our shopping malls are now open for business on Sundays, but that was not the case in Israel. Times of worship were still days of rest from labor in Israel — days when everyone could enjoy the cessation from work that God gave in his mercy from the beginning (cf. Exodus 20:8-11; 23:12; 34:21, etc.). And that the merchants of ancient Israel did not approve. They muttered over the New Moon festival rests at the beginning of every month, and they did not like every seventh day sabbath of rest. They wanted to sell and accumulate money. They were very much like us.

More than that, the merchants of the northern kingdom were so intent on adding to their wealth that they cheated those who bought from them. They made the *ephah*, that forty-liter measure of grain, smaller than its standard, and they made the *shekel*, the 11.5 gram weight on the balance scale, heavier so that more silver would have to be paid to them. They even bent the balance scale out of shape in order to cheat their customers.

The result was that poor people in their society could not afford to buy food without falling into debt and being sold into slavery. With their ill-gotten gain, the cheating merchants could buy slaves for as little as a price of sandals, while some of the poor were reduced to scraping up the chaff and leavings on the threshing floor in order to have something to eat (v. 6).

All such practices violated Israel's law. From the earliest times, such dishonesty was specifically forbidden in the Torah (Leviticus 19:35-36; Deuteronomy 25:13-16) as an "abomination" to the Lord (Proverbs 11:1; 16:11; 20:10, 23). "You shall not steal," God commanded in the Decalogue (Exodus 20:15). Israel's sellers defied God's covenant command.

207

God, however, does not pass over our sinful ways or ignore our neglect of his just commands. In our text, he swears by "the pride of Jacob," ironically taking an oath by Israel's proud self-confidence (cf. Amos 5:18—6:14). God will not forget his people's sin, and as is announced at the beginning of Amos 8, an "end" will come upon Israel for her actions (cf. 7:8; 8:2). Her ten northern tribes will be carried into Assyrian exile in 721 B.C. and disappear from history. God will have done with their defiance of his lordship.

Proper 21

Jeremiah 32:1-3a, 6-15

The time is 588 B.C. in our text. Jerusalem is under siege by the troops of Babylonia, and Jeremiah is imprisoned in the court of the palace guard. He is a traitor to the government of King Zedekiah, because he has been preaching that it is the will of God that Judah surrender to the Babylonians.

If one reads of the conditions in Jerusalem during the siege, the situation is appalling. Jeremiah (19:9), Ezekiel (5:10), and Lamentations (2:12, 19-20; 4:4, 7-10) all tell us that toward the end of the siege, parents were eating the flesh of their children. Epidemics and disease swept through the weakened and crowded population. Material property was of no value. Silver and gold were worthless, because there was nothing to buy. All commercial enterprises collapsed because there was nothing to sell. Property values plummeted, as they always do in war, because everyone was trying to sell property and to flee the city. Who wanted any land when the Babylonians were knocking at the gates?

It is in this situation that the Word of the Lord comes to Jeremiah. "Buy the field which is at Anathoth in the land of Benjamin, for the right of possession and redemption is yours. Buy it for yourself. Then I knew," declares the prophet, "that this was the word of the Lord."

The command is totally incomprehensible to Jeremiah, as we read in verses 24-25. Jeremiah knows that Jerusalem is going to fall because of its rebellion against God. And yet Jeremiah is told, send and buy a field. When everything looks hopeless! When fields and farms are not worth a penny. When there seems to be no hope, because the world is crumbling about us, and the only thing worth doing seems to be to survive by any means here and now, and never mind the consequences. When our terrible, weak, blind human failures have got us into this mess, and we can no longer stand to analyze the guilty past or to look forward to the awful future that we have determined for ourselves. When we try to shut out memory, shut out hope, and just try to stay alive.

But the word is not, Guard what you have, Jeremiah. Hide your scraps of bread and your cup of water from those who peer hungrily into your courtyard. Never mind what's happening outside in the street. Look out for yourself. No. The word is: Buy a field. And the reason for that command to the prophet is given in verse 15. "For thus says the Lord of hosts, the God of Israel: Houses and fields and vineyards shall again be bought in this land."

That is the Word of God that comes to us from this passage in Jeremiah. When everything is hopeless on our human scene, God still has a plan for the future.

When we stand beside the grave of a loved one, and all the pain floods over us; when we realize that we can never more say what we wanted to say and can never more do what we wanted to do for that loved one, God has a plan.

When everything lovely and gracious and pure in our world seems to fall victim to corruption and evil; when no good work seems to endure, and no project of love seems to bear lasting fruit; when everything we do is tainted by selfishness, God has a plan.

When the meek, the peacemakers, the pure in heart, get trampled into the dirt; when the weak constantly are sacrificed on the altars of power, and the tongues of the proud and mighty strut through the earth, God has a plan.

When there seems to lie ahead of us nothing but a crucifixion; when the Gethsemane of prayer is darkened by the shadow of a looming Golgotha; when we would rather do any other thing than obey the will of the Father, and we cry out to him to remove this cup from us, God has a plan.

It is a plan of love to save us and our world, despite the fact that we deserve nothing but God's condemnation of death. It is a plan to recreate that good and abundant and eternal life on earth that God intended for his world in the beginning. It is a plan to make a new people, a new community, that knows how to live together in justice and peace and righteousness, under the lordship of God. And in Jeremiah, we see God patiently, step by step, working out that plan for the future that will finally lead to a cross, a resurrection, an ascension, and the gift of the Holy Spirit to us all.

Lutheran Option: Amos 6:1a, 4-7

This judgment oracle is the second in a series of three in which Amos attacks those things in which the eighth century northern kingdom of Israel places her confidence and security (Amos 5:18—6:14). Significantly the section begins with an announcement of the coming Day of the Lord, the day of God's final judgment on his people (5:18-20), that will be darkness and not light because of Israel's continuing violation of God's order for the covenant community. The people place their confidence in their lavish worship rituals (5:21-24), in their wealth (6:1-7), and in their military might (6:8-11), and the prophet declares that all of those guarantees of security will be useless before God's judgment (6:12-14).

Our particular text concerns the ill-placed confidence that Israel's leaders have in their wealth (cf. Isaiah 2:20-21). The lectionary has wisely eliminated verses 2 and 3, because those are probably inserts from the later time when the cities named fell to the Assyrians. The remaining verses have the form of a Woe Oracle, that is, of a funeral lament for one who is dead, presaging Israel's future ruin.

The picture given of the wealthy in Israel's society is vivid. The upper crust, "the notable men," consider themselves to be leaders of "the first of the nations," the most important and powerful kingdom on earth — a sarcastic address on Amos' part. While the southern kingdom is mentioned ("Zion"), it is only for purposes of comparison. In the north, in Israel, are found the leaders of the world — or so they think. And it is their wealth that gives them that delusion.

After all, God has blessed them. They are able to sprawl about at their banquets on couches inlaid with costly ivory. They can eat the choicest meats, although meat of any kind was a rarity in Israel. They can amuse themselves by improvising songs (the Hebrew calls it "screechings") on lutes and timbrels. They can intoxicate themselves with wine drunk not from cups, but from bowls. And they can stimulate themselves by anointing their skin with fragrant oils. All the luxuries of life are theirs. So surely they live in the favor of God, because he has poured out innumerable blessings upon them. It is a confidence not unknown to us well-to-do in American society.

Yet, these rich leaders of Israel lack the most important gift — the gift of concern for the "ruin of Joseph" (v. 6), compassion for those less well-off, anger over the injustice taking place in their courts and commerce, zeal for the will of God for their society. Secure, comfortable, able to have and to do anything they want, these so-called notable, well-fed, well-off people give no thought either to the Lord or to their neighbors. Is that not a description of many of us so much of the time?

But God gives thought to them — and to us. And so those who are "first" in the "first of the nations" will indeed be "first" — first into Assyrian exile (v. 7). Those comforts and that power in which they place their trust will be useless to turn aside the judgment of the Lord of all upon them. For there is only One who can give us true security, no matter what our station in life. There is only One who can mark out for us the way to a truly just society. And there is only One whom we can trust to preserve our lives, though heaven and earth pass away. The psalmist sings it well. "God is our refuge and strength ... Therefore we will not fear" (Psalm 46:1, 2). In God and his will for human beings, though we be rich or poor or middle-class, important or useful or insignificant, lie all our hope, our preservation, and our good.

Proper 22

Lamentations 1:1-6

We are uncomfortable with tears and lamenting, aren't we? If someone breaks into tears, we try our best to get her to stop crying and to smile again. Or if an acquaintance has experienced some awful calamity, sometimes we don't even know what to say to him. Or if we do attempt to comfort, we try to assure that everything will work out for the best in the end.

We do not like sorrow. We either try to avoid it or we attempt to do away with it. And so a lot of preaching these days is simply therapeutic comfort, designed to make the worshipers feel good about themselves. Our religion, we think, should deal with the happy side of life and make us feel better. It should not be connected with lamenting and loss.

The scriptures, however, know better. The Bible is the most realistic book in the world. And so the authors of our Bible make a wide place in their writings for the sorrows and sufferings and pains of human life, because they know that those are part of our daily living and that there is a word from God about those experiences too.

In our text, which is made up of the first six verses of an acrostic poem, Jerusalem is pictured as a woman mourning over the death of her husband. The city was destroyed by the Babylonians in 587 B.C., and she who was a great princess among the nations has become a vassal slave to Babylonia. Betrayed by her allies and friends, she has no one to comfort her. Her children, that is, the population, has been taken into exile. Her leaders were exiled already in the deportation of 597 B.C. And even the roads to Zion are pictured as mourning, because no one now traverses them for the great pilgrimage feasts of Tabernacles, Passover, and Weeks.

Our text is very clear about the reason for Jerusalem's destruction. "The Lord," we read in verse 5, "has made her suffer for the multitude of her transgressions." As in the prophecies of Jeremiah and Ezekiel, Jerusalem and Judah have fallen to the foreign conqueror, because they have turned away from their God, broken their covenant with him, ignored his commandments for the order of their daily living, trusted in their own strength for security, and given their allegiance to the pagan fertility gods of other nations.

But the Holy One of Israel is a God whose lordship over all nations cannot be ignored. And when Judah tries to be free of that lordship, she is subjected to God's penalty. As it is written in Ezekiel, "As I live, says the Lord God, surely with a mighty hand and an outstretched arm, and with wrath poured out, I will be king over you" (Ezekiel 20:33). The Lord is King over our lives, and we ignore that kingship at our peril. "God is not mocked," writes Paul, "for whatever a man sows, that he will also reap" (Galatians 6:7). And as our text shows, that applies not only to individual lives, but to the lives of nations as well. God allowed the Babylonians to destroy Jerusalem, because Judah had deserted her covenant with her Lord.

We squirm at those words, and they make us feel very uncomfortable. But they are words embedded in the actual history of Judah, who suffered for her sins against her God, just as they are also words embedded in our histories that are so pocked with suffering, because we ignore our God. All suffering and afflictions do not come from God's hand. Sometimes they are just the consequences of our own foolish actions. And God is very, very slow to bring distress upon us — he is "slow to anger," says the prophet Nahum (1:3). The Bible tells us that he is more grieved than angry at our unrighteous ways (cf. Genesis 6:5). But can any one of us here this morning doubt that we also often suffer some blow, because we have not followed God's will for our lives? How often has our sin got us into some deep difficulty!

Our text from Lamentations is very instructive, then, on that score, because Jerusalem's lament in this text also leads her into confession that she has been wrong in turning from her God (cf. 1:18, 20, 22). And that is the first step on the way to forgiveness and to healing. God's judgments upon us are never meant to destroy us, as Judah and Jerusalem were not forever destroyed. Rather,

God's judgments are meant to bring us to our senses, so that we seek the renewal of life that is found in turning from our sinful ways and committing ourselves anew to our Lord. "If we confess our sins, he is faithful and just, and will forgive our sins and cleanse us from all unrighteousness" (1 John 1:9). Indeed, God loves us so much and wants good for us so very, very much, that he gives his only begotten Son to forgive us and to give us new life. Troubles with their lamenting and tears can issue in joy, if they take us through repentance and turning to the Lord.

Lutheran Option: Habakkuk 1:1-4; 2:1-4

Do you ever grow weary of the constant struggle with evil? Every time we read a newspaper, we see that someone else has been murdered or robbed, or that young people have fallen victim to drugs and outlandish sexual exploits, or that some person in the government has been found to be a crook. Violence, chaos, evil seem to surround us on every side in our society. Indeed, even in our schools and churches, chaos seems to reign. Young people are not taught, scandals stain the ministry, and far from faithfulness to God, everyone seems just to be doing his or her own thing.

We seem helpless, moreover, to do anything about it. As our text in Habakkuk says, "The wicked surround the righteous," and when decent people try to restore order and goodness to our lives, they seem to get drowned out by the indecent. It makes us wonder just what our world is coming to.

That was the prophet Habakkuk's situation, too. In 598 B.C., that Judean prophet saw on every side wrongs, destruction, violence, and he cried out in anguish, "How long, O Lord?" How long are you going to put up with this state of affairs?

God replied to the prophet that the Babylonians were going to invade Judah and wipe out all her wrongs (1:5-11). But the Babylonians were even worse in their evil than Judah was and that didn't seem like much of a solution (1:12-17). So Habakkuk set himself to watch and listen to what God would say to him, like a man stationing himself on a watchtower. Habakkuk concentrated his prayers and attention on God. And God replied to him, as God always replies to sincere prayer (2:1-4).

The vision is coming, God told his prophet. It may seem slow in coming to you, but it is hastening in its progress, and it will surely come. In short, God assured Habakkuk that the kingdom of heaven would surely become reality — that kingdom in which violence and evil are done away, and there is no pain or crying or death anymore; that kingdom in which God himself will wipe away all our tears and dwell forever in our midst.

The Kingdom of God is coming. Indeed, it began to come in the person of Jesus Christ, when he began his ministry and announced, "The time is fulfilled. The Kingdom of God is at hand. Repent and believe in the gospel" (Mark 1:15). God's new age of goodness has broken into human history, and it will come in its fullness, and evil and violence and death will be no more when Christ returns to be with us. Such is the certain hope of the scriptures and of the Christian Church. The evil we experience in our world is not the last word. God's Word, incarnate in Jesus Christ, will be all in all (cf. Ephesians 1:10).

In our meantime, therefore, while you and I await the coming of the kingdom in its fullness, God's word from our text tells us that if we will be steadfast in our faithfulness, we can live with whatever happens in the world around us. If we are puffed up and proud and try to go it on our own, we will fail. But if we persistently and continually cling to God, we cannot be defeated. Verse 4 of our text has often been read, "The righteous shall live by faith." But the word for faith is 'emunah in the Hebrew, from which comes our word "amen," and which has the meaning of steadfastness, day by day putting one foot in front of another to walk in God's ways and not our own. If we will be thus faithful, we will live, both now and in the eternal kingdom that is coming.

Proper 23

Jeremiah 29:1, 4-7

The prominent people, the "best" people of Judah, were carried into Babylonian exile in the first deportation of 597 B.C., but they really didn't think their captivity would last too long. After all, they had the davidic king, Jehoiachin, with them, and God had promised that there would never be lacking a davidic king to sit upon the throne (2 Samuel 7). Their prophets had always prophesied "peace, peace" to them (Jeremiah 6:14; 8:11), which meant God held them in favor. And now the same prophets, who also had been deported, were assuring them that they would soon be returned to Palestine.

They all looked to Egypt to break the power of Babylonia. In fact, when there was a rebellion in the Babylonian army in 595 B.C., they were sure that was going to bear fruit. In 594, ambassadors from Edom, Moab, Ammon, Tyre, and Sidon met in Jerusalem to plot how to regain their freedom from the Babylonian yoke. And when Psammetichus II took the throne of Egypt in 593, that seemed the most hopeful sign of all.

What the exiled leaders did not reckon with, however, was the power of God that was far greater than the power of any little nation, and far greater than that of Egypt and of Babylonia. And God had sent the Judean leaders into their exile, because they had trusted everything else but him, giving their allegiance to other gods, other powers, other ways than that of the Lord.

The result was that the puppet king Zedekiah of Judah, whom Babylonia had put on the throne, had to send a deputation to Babylonia in 593 B.C., assuring its Emperor Nebuchadnezzar that Judah was a faithful vassal. And the prophet Jeremiah seized the opportunity to have that deputation carry a letter to the exiles.

Do not believe your false prophets who are telling you that you will soon return to your homeland, Jeremiah told the deportees.

Settle down for a long stay. Build houses, plant gardens, intermarry with the Babylonians, and pray for Babylon's welfare, for your life is bound up with hers for the next seventy years (vv. 5-10). At a time when Babylonia was hated and feared throughout the Near East, to a nation that had never countenanced intermarriage with foreigners (cf. Genesis 28:1), and to Judeans who thought that God could be found only in Jerusalem, that was a revolutionary message. Indeed, it was a treasonous message, and one of the priests among the exiles wrote to King Zedekiah to have Jeremiah silenced (vv. 24-28). But unlike the other false prophets who preached only peace and weal, Jeremiah preached the Word of the Lord. He knew that the Lord was in charge of Judah's life, and that only the Lord could give Judah "a future and a hope" (vv. 10-11).

In the affairs of nations, as empires rise and fall, as politicians plot and plan and think to shape our futures, there is One who is finally in charge of our destinies. That is a message to remember in our century when we think everyone but God is in control. And so the final question we always must ask, the question that exiled Judah did not ask, was: How do we stand with our God? And surely our nation, along with Judah, would have to find itself unfaithful.

Perhaps the most amazing aspect of Jeremiah's letter, however, is its destruction of all nationalistic bounds. God was not bound to one nation, to one temple, to one people, Jeremiah proclaimed, any more than he is bound to the United States or our denomination or our western ways. God is the Lord over all nations. He can be found in the midst of the third world as readily as in the midst of our great nation. He is not bound to our ways of worship or our understandings of piety and ethics. He works his will among all peoples and can be found in their midst, if he is sought with all our hearts and minds (vv. 13-14).

Most important, the Lord is to be sought after in whatever situation we find ourselves. And Jeremiah proclaims that we serve the Lord by serving those around us, even if they be our enemies or hated by us or looked down upon. The scriptures have always proclaimed that we love God most sincerely by loving our neighbors, whoever they may be. For the God of the scriptures is always giving away that which belongs to him. If you love me, he teaches us, then give that love to those around you. And in doing that, you will be giving your devotion to me.

Lutheran Option: 2 Kings 5:1-3, 7-15c

There is no doubt about it. Naaman, the commander of the army of the King of Syria, is a very important person. In fact, he is a national hero, noted for his victories and for his courage and daring in times of war. Each time he comes home from battle, he is celebrated and honored by the populace and by his king.

Like all persons of whatever station in life, however, Naaman suffers "the slings and arrows of outrageous fortune." He has a progressive disease. He is a leper. Nevertheless, contrary to the treatment given to most lepers, Naaman expects to be afforded the respect proper to his high station. He hears from his wife through her little Israelite slave girl that there is a prophet in northern Israel who can cure him. But does Naaman write to the prophet? No. He writes to the king of Israel. And when he arrives in his chariot, with all of his entourage, at the door of Elisha, he expects Elisha to come out to him and, through great ceremony, to cure him of his disease. Important people need to be treated in an important fashion.

Those who are of God do not pay much attention to human importance, however. How often that was the case with Jesus! And it is also the case with Elisha. He just sends a messenger out to Naaman to tell him to wash in the Jordan seven times in order to be cured. Naaman is furious. He has been treated like some peasant, like some scum who has no status whatsoever. His honor, his high station in life, his military victories have been ignored, and he has been treated like anyone else. What a come-down!

But Elisha knows, and his lowly servants know, and above all, God knows, that the path to Naaman's wholeness lies down the way of humility. Naaman not only needs to get rid of his leprosy. He needs to get rid of himself. "Whoever exalts himself will be humbled, and whoever humbles himself will be exalted," our Lord taught us (Matthew 23:12). When we're all wrapped up in ourselves, there is no room left for God. We are the most important

219

person in our lives, when in actuality, God is to be that Person. That is the reason Jesus tells us to "take up our cross" and follow him. In short, we are to let ourselves — our wills, our desires, our importance — be crucified, that Christ may live in us and God may be our all in all.

The Lord granted wholeness to Naaman when he found and exercised humility, when he finally realized that he had no health in himself and that his life lay wholly in God's hands. And we too have our wholeness from God, no matter what our condition, when we renounce our own self-importance and let God have his way with our lives.

Proper 24

Jeremiah 31:27-34

The lectionary has included two separate oracles in this reading, verses 27-30 and verses 31-34. The first includes a quotation from Ezekiel 18:2 and is probably a later addition to the genuine oracles of the prophet. Nevertheless, it picks up a theme from Jeremiah's call. Judah languishes in Babylonian exile. God has plucked up and broken down, overthrown and destroyed (Jeremiah 1:10), because of his people's faithlessness toward him. But now God will build and plant in Judah's future. Judgment is never God's last word.

The promise of the new covenant that follows in verses 31-34 forms God's solution to Israel's sinfulness. God had held out the invitation to his people to mend their ways and to return to him. But they would not. To every gracious invitation from God, they replied, "That is vain. We will follow our own plans and will every one act according to the stubbornness of his evil heart" (Jeremiah 18:12). In fact, they not only rejected God's grace, but mocked his word and persecuted his prophet. Their sin had such a grip on them that they no longer had any power of self-assessment (cf. Jeremiah 8:4-7), and finally, they had no power in themselves to repent and return (cf. Hosea 5:4). "Can the Ethiopian change his skin or the leopard his spots?" God asked. "Then also you can do good who are accustomed to do evil" (Jeremiah 13:23). Israel's sin was written with the point of a diamond on her heart, replacing God's word that was supposed to be there (Jeremiah 17:1; Deuteronomy 6:6).

The history of Israel's sin is reviewed in verses 31-32 of our text. Despite God's grace — despite the fact that he took his people by the hand and led them, like a father his son, out of captivity in Egypt and made a covenant with them at Sinai, and then renewed that covenant with them in the Deuteronomic reform of 621 B.C. — despite the whole long history of God's mercy toward his covenant people — they nevertheless broke covenant faithfulness with him. He was their husband — to use the figure in the text — the one who had so tenderly loved them in the wilderness (Jeremiah 2:2). Yet Israel whored after other lovers (Jeremiah 2:23-25) and gave her devotion to other gods and goddesses (Jeremiah 7:17-18, 30-31). God therefore rejected them as his people and sent them into exile (Jeremiah 12:7).

When we read the account of Israel's inability to see her own sinfulness and to repent, we find a very accurate description of our sin too, do we not? We sinners do not see ourselves as God sees us. We think we are righteous people who do good most of the time. We rationalize our faithless ways, excuse our shortcomings, consider our day-by-day commitment to other goals and loves, rather than to the love of God, as necessary to our lives. Or when we do earnestly try to follow God's will and to do the good, we find that we always fall short, secretly looking out for our own interests instead of for the interests of God and neighbor. In Paul's words, "We are slaves of sin" (Romans 6), unable to do the good that we would, and doing the evil that we do not want (Romans 7:19). We are captive to our selfishness, our pride, our anxieties for our own well-being. Such was the nature of Israel's life in Jeremiah's time, and such is still the nature of ours.

A merciful God did not give up on Israel, however, and he does not give up on us. Instead, God here in our text adopts the one solution for sin that is possible. He announces that he will make a new covenant with his people Israel. He will in the future change his people's sinful hearts (cf. Ezekiel 36:26-27), transforming them from the inside out, because it is from our hearts that our sin comes forth (cf. Mark 7:21-23). In place of the sin written on Israel's heart, God will write the words of his law or teaching, enabling the people to obey him in faithfulness and in love (cf. Deuteronomy 6:4-6). Their sinful past will be forgotten — God will forgive it all — and they will be reunited with him in a new covenant relationship of devotion and gratitude and obedience. Indeed, so thorough will be God's transformation of the hearts of his people that no one will have to teach his or her neighbor about the character of God. All will know him, in an intimate relationship like that of a faithful wife with her husband. All will cleave to him and follow him and love him with all their being. What his people could not do for themselves, God will do for them in an act of pure mercy and love.

Such was the promise that God made for Israel's future. But like everything in the Old Testament, we have to ask, Did God keep his promise? What happened to these ancient words? Were they fulfilled, or were they allowed to disappear into the forgotten mists of time?

The testimony of the New Testament is that God kept this ancient promise to his covenant folk. "The Lord Jesus on the night that he was betrayed took bread ... In the same way also the cup, after supper, saying, 'This cup is the new covenant in my blood' " (1 Corinthians 11:23-25; cf. Matthew 26:28; Mark 14:24; Luke 22:20). God replaced his old covenant, which his people broke, with his new covenant in Jesus Christ and thereby made it possible for his covenant people to live new lives of faithfulness and obedience (cf. Hebrews 8:8-12; 10:16-17).

God has written this new covenant upon our hearts by the work of the Holy Spirit, testifies Paul (cf. Romans 5:5). He has sent the Spirit of his Son into our hearts, so that we are no longer slaves but heirs (Galatians 4:6-7). He "has shone in our hearts to give the light of the knowledge of the glory of God in the face of Christ" (2 Corinthians 4:6). Christians therefore now can live the new life of the Spirit (Romans 7:6). Though we were once slaves of sin, we now can be obedient from the heart to the will of God (Romans 6:17). In short, Christians now have the possibility not to sin — not by their own power, but solely by the power of God working in them. "Let not sin therefore reign in your mortal bodies," Paul admonishes us (Romans 6:12), and by the power of Jesus Christ, lent to us in the Spirit, we can follow that admonition. We can in truth become new creations in Jesus Christ (2 Corinthians 5:17) and lead a new life of faithfulness.

Like so much in the Old Testament, Jeremiah's promise of a new covenant finds its fulfillment in the New. However, the fulfillment is "already," but it is also "not yet." It is not complete. We have been made new creations in Christ, but our perfect obedience awaits that time when the Spirit, given us as a guarantee (cf. 2 Corinthians 1:22; 5:5; Ephesians 1:14), changes us wholly into the image of Christ (2 Corinthians 3:18), and we are presented before the Father "without spot or wrinkle or any such thing ... holy and without blemish" (Ephesians 5:27). Similarly, our Jewish brothers and sisters await that blessed time when "all Israel will be saved," (Romans 11:26) and we all are joined together in God's one covenant fellowship in Christ.

There is also a missionary message in this new covenant passage that must not be overlooked by us Christians. Its promise is that all people will know the Lord, "from the least of them to the greatest." But all people have not yet, in faith, received the Spirit of Christ into their hearts. And so we who, by the mercy of God, have been grafted into the new covenant as members of the "commonwealth of Israel" (Ephesians 2:12), are sent into all the world to proclaim the glad news that new life and goodness and eternal life with God are possible through faith in Jesus Christ our Lord.

Proper 25, Reformation Sunday

Joel 2:23-32

The lectionary sometimes begins a reading in the middle of one oracle and adds to it another. That is true of the Old Testament text for this Reformation Day. Joel 2:23-27 are the second half of the poem that begins in 2:18. Joel 2:28-32 then constitutes a separate oracle.

To understand this lesson, we really need to understand the whole message of Joel. In the post-exilic fourth century B.C., Judah experiences a devastating locust plague, followed by a drought (1:1-14). Joel never states explicitly the nature of Judah's sin, although he probably has Judah's apostasy in mind. But Joel's warning to his compatriots is that an even greater judgment is coming upon them for their violation of their covenant, a judgment that will affect the whole cosmos — the judgment of the Day of the Lord, when God comes to set up his kingdom on earth (1:15—2:11).

Out of pure grace, through the message of Joel, God nevertheless holds out to his apostate people the opportunity to repent and to return in faithfulness to their covenant with their Lord (2:12-17). But no matter what Judah's response is — and it is not recorded — God goes on to tell his people the marvelous things he will do for them, simply out of the pity that he has in his heart for his beloved people (2:18). That telling makes up verses 23-27 of our stated text.

In his grace, God will restore to Judah all that they have lost in the locust plague and drought. The ground will be restored (cf. 2:21 with 1:10). The wild animals will be fed (cf. 2:22 with 1:20). Joy will return to Judah's harvests and worship (cf. 2:23 with 1:16). The drought will be a thing of the past (cf. 2:23 with 1:10, 12, 18-20). The fruit trees will bear (cf. 2:22 with 1:12, 19). Threshing floors and wine vats will be full (cf. 2:24 with 1:5, 17). All are blessings in the covenant relation that God will reestablish with his people (cf. Deuteronomy 11:12-17; 28:3-5, 11-12; Leviticus 26:3-5), and all make up the blessed future into which God will lead his chosen folk.

Best of all, in such promised future, Israel will know that the Lord is in her midst and that he alone is God (2:27). Her apostate past will be behind her. She will be reunited with her Lord.

We should note well, however, on this Reformation Sunday. Such a blessed future is not the reward of any action or repentance on sinful Judah's part, but simply the outpouring of the grace of the God, who above all else wishes abundant life for his own.

By joining 2:28-29 with 2:27, our text makes the point that Judah's reunion with her God will be manifested in his gift of the spirit to all flesh. Probably the words "all flesh" refer to all persons in Judah, since that is what is emphasized in the following lines. All of God's covenant people will enjoy the intimate relation with him hitherto known only to the prophets. God will be with them in their midst; they will know him; and they will worship him alone, in covenant faithfulness.

Joel 2:28-29 are those verses that are quoted by Peter in Acts 2:17-18 on the day of Pentecost, when the church is given the gift of God's Spirit, and in that event, the gift of the Spirit is indeed afforded to "all flesh" of every nation. Now all peoples everywhere can live in covenant communion with the Lord.

Nevertheless, as Joel 2:30-32 and Acts 2:19-21 record, the Day of the Lord, when he returns to judge all flesh, still comes. And once again, Joel — and indeed Peter — issue a warning. It is possible to be given the gift of the Spirit of God and to do nothing with him. We can let the Spirit lie dormant within our hearts. We can ignore his promptings and follow our own desires. We can even deny that God has entered our hearts at all. But, as the New Testament affirms in the parables and teachings of Jesus and in the writings of Paul, we shall all stand before the judgment seat of God in the Day that comes.

God, in his mercy, will give us a signal before the day is upon us, however (cf. Malachi 4:5; Luke 21:25-28). As in the apocalyptic passages of Mark 13, Matthew 24, and Luke 21, there will be signs in heaven and on earth. Joel lists blood and fire and columns of smoke from burning cities, and the sun darkened and the moon turned to blood (Joel 2:30-31), not from an eclipse or sandstorm as some would have it, but by God.

As Joel proclaims, and as Peter (Acts 2:21) and Paul (Romans 10:13) both pronounce, however, those who call upon the name of the Lord shall be delivered from destruction (Joel 2:31). We need to ask, therefore, what that means.

Certainly the prophet and apostles do not have in mind some last minute plea for mercy, some prayer uttered simply to save our own skins. To be sure, there is more joy in heaven over one sinner who repents than over 99 righteous persons who need no repentance (Luke 15:7). But true repentance and turning to the Lord involve not the effort to save ourselves, but the humble deliverance of all we are into God's hands to do with as he will (cf. the Gospel lesson for the day).

Indeed, if we let the scripture interpret the scripture and look up other passages in which we find the phrase "to call on the name of the Lord," we find that it involves a rich and persistent life of devotion to God. It means to worship God (Genesis 12:8), to acknowledge that we belong to him alone (Isaiah 12:2-4; 44:5; Psalm 105:1; Zechariah 13:9), and to depend on him for all life and good (Proverbs 18:10). All of that involves not just one act of commitment, but the day-by-day attempt to let God rule our lives — repeated repentance that issues in continual devotion and communion with our Lord.

Further, "to call on the name of the Lord" is, throughout the scriptures, to tell others what God has done (cf. Psalm 105;1; Isaiah 12:4) — as Acts emphasizes, to be the Lord's witnesses to the end of the earth (Acts 1:8). Thus it is that Paul quotes "Everyone who calls upon the name of the Lord will be saved" (Romans 10:13). But then he goes on to ask how persons can call on the Lord of whom they have never heard, and how can they hear without a preacher or a witness to tell them the good news. So Christians are summoned, as they call on God for salvation, to invite all others into that blessed life.

Finally, our text from Joel states that those who call on God for deliverance are those whom God has already called (Joel 2:32).

That is always the way it is in the scriptures. God's act is always first, God's grace is always "prevenient." And the implication is that those who have been given the Spirit, as in verses 28 and 29, are those who are enabled to worship and serve and witness.

So the message from Joel is very clear. We Christians are those who have been given the Spirit of the Lord at our baptisms. In the power of that Spirit, we are enabled to "call on the name of the Lord," with all that phrase implies. Therefore, when Christ returns on the Day of the Lord "to judge the quick and the dead," we need have no fear (2:21, 22). Indeed, God holds out before us an abundant life analogous to that of which we read in Joel 2:23-27, with God in our midst (2:27) and great gladness and joy in his presence (2:23).

Lutheran Option: Jeremiah 31:31-34

See the exposition for the previous Sunday.

All Saints' Sunday

Daniel 7:1-3, 15-18

Do you ever feel like giving up on your Christian faith? It is never easy to lead a Christian life — never let anyone tell you differently. But perhaps in our time, it seems even more difficult than ever. We are surrounded by a society in which all truth seems to have been lost, and everything is relative, depending on individual opinion. Selfishness and commercialism rule the day. Right and wrong are no longer remarked. Power and pleasure have become the goals. And God can be anything someone imagines. Indeed, even some of our churches seem to have lost their bearing, with no agreement on their theology and ethics and their worship infected with pagan rituals.

To withstand all of that, to cling to the worship of the one true God, to shape our lives according to his commandments, and to defy the scorn of a secular society is no easy task. After all, even the media has characterized evangelical Christians as ignorant, misguided, and easily led. Faithful Christians are a minority in our world, and like all minorities, sometimes they have to suffer for what they are.

There are Christians around the world who are still dying for their faith and practice — in China, in Central America, in Africa. And while we comfortable Americans rarely suffer because we easily accommodate ourselves to the culture around us, those who try to be faithful to the Lord know that it is no easy task.

It was no easy task in the second century B.C., when the book of Daniel was written. The remnant of what had been the people of Judah lived in the Hellenistic Empire, under the thumb of Antiochus IV Epiphanes. And that ruler was so tyrannical that he persecuted the Jews and deliberately defiled their temple by sacrificing a pig on its altar.

Daniel therefore was written to strengthen those Jews in their faith in a time of persecution and to assure them that if they held fast to their faith to the end, their reward would be great in heaven. The first six chapters of the book recount stories of faithful courage and obedience that could give examples of perseverance in the face of suffering to those who were being persecuted. Chapters 8 through 12 are visions of the overthrow and judgment of the persecuting tyrants, and of the glory that awaits the faithful. Chapter 7, with our text for the day, forms the heart of the book.

Daniel is given the vision in chapter 7 of four great beasts rising out of the sea. They symbolize the Babylonian, Median, Persian, and Hellenistic Empires, to which the Jews have been subject since the sixth century B.C. The eleventh little horn that grows up from the fourth beast is Antiochus.

Verses 9-14 of chapter 7 portray the Day of Judgment at the end of history, when the beasts are judged by God, who is called "the Ancient of Days," and who appears in his fiery chariot (cf. Ezekiel 1:15-28). He opens the heavenly books and decrees the death of the eleventh little horn, while the rest of the beasts are stripped of their rule and held in captivity. Then comes "one like a son of man," to whom is given everlasting "dominion and glory" and the rule over all "peoples, nations, and languages" in a kingdom that will not pass away.

Finally, in verses 15-28, an angel interprets the vision for Daniel, and from our particular text, verses 15-18, we learn that the "one like a son of man" is a corporate figure representing "the saints of the Most High" (vv. 18, 22, 17), that is, the faithful Jews who persevere under persecution to the end. In a short time, the book is saying (v. 25), dominion will be taken away from the hands of the tyrant and given to the saints in the faith, who will rule forever.

What are we to make of all of that? Certainly we are not to use Daniel to try to predict events in our future. Daniel is an apocalypse, written in a particular time, to strengthen and encourage those being persecuted in its own age. Its bizarre language is intended to mislead the governing authorities. But its principal purpose is directed toward its own time and place.

Nevertheless, the message of Daniel is pertinent for all Christians everywhere. God is the Ruler over all of the tyrants and evils of history, Daniel proclaims. And those who cling to God, no matter what their circumstance, and who hold fast to their faith in the Lord to the end, will receive a glorious reward from their God. They will become members of that heavenly company of faithful — the communion of saints — who reign on high with the Lord God.

The New Testament's use of Daniel alters its understanding to a certain extent. During his ministry, Jesus repeatedly uses the title Son of Man to refer to himself, drawing on the use of that term in later Jewish apocalypticism (1 Enoch; 2 Esdras), probably for the purpose of obscuring his identity as the Messiah. But our Lord does, like Daniel, assure those who are faithful in this life that their reward will be great in eternity.

> *Blessed are you when men hate you, and when they exclude you and revile you, and cast out your name as evil, on account of the Son of Man! Rejoice in that day and leap for joy, for behold, your reward is great in heaven; for so their fathers did to the prophets.*
>
> Luke 6:22-23

Matthew even mentions that the faithful will share in the rule of Christ (Matthew 19:28). And Paul sees a glorious future for the saints in heaven (Romans 8:7; 1 Corinthians 1:12; cf. 2 Timothy 2:11-12; Ephesians 1:18; Acts 26:18).

Whatever language the New Testament writers borrow to describe eternal life — and they seem to strain at the boundaries of language — their assurance is that the life of the communion of saints will be glorious. Those who remain faithful to their Lord Jesus Christ will be with him, sharing in his good eternity, recipients of his everlasting love and life.

So the message of Daniel endures and, like the entire Old Testament, finds its final formulation and fulfillment in Christ for those who trust in him. As Jesus taught us, "In the world you may have tribulation; but be of good cheer, I have overcome the world" (John 16:33). And his cheer, his joy, his victory, his kingdom, will be given to those who hold fast to him.

Proper 27

Haggai 1:15b — 2:9

A cynic once remarked that Jesus came preaching the Kingdom of God, and what he got was the church — a distinct disappointment. Certainly there is reason to be disappointed with the church these days. Its membership is melting away. Its life is torn by controversy and dissent. Its influence on the life of society has all but disappeared. And those who have found the center of their trust in the church's message, through all their life long, despair of the slow ruin to which it seems to be subject.

After all, there was a day when the church counted for something in this country. Its buildings dominated every urban skyscape. Its preachers were among the noted figures in the populace. Its acts of mercy were known throughout the world. Its ethics guided society's customs and laws. And even *The New York Times* featured reviews of its sermons and programs. But now all that glory seems a thing of the past, and the church sometimes appears in our eyes as insignificant and helpless.

The populace in Haggai's time had much the same feeling about the temple on Zion that was being rebuilt. The date of our text is given exactly: October 17, 520 B.C. The people have returned from their exile in Babylonia to form a little congregation under the rule of Darius I, Hystaspes of Persia. They are allowed to have their own governor, the davidic Zerubbabel, and their own high priest, Joshua the son of Zehozadak. But they are struggling and desperately poor. Drought has stunted their crops and brought widespread hunger. Inflation has eaten into their meager earnings. Jerusalem still lies mostly in ruins. But Haggai the prophet has urged them to rebuild the temple of the Lord, and one month earlier they laid the foundation of that sanctuary.

The result of the rebuilding is pitiful, however. The Hebrew of our text calls it "much more than nothing" (v. 3) an insignificant little structure compared to the temple of Solomon that once stood on the site. When the old folks see what the rebuilt temple is going to look like, they weep, for they remember so well the glorious structure that went before: the first temple's cedar and cypress, gold and carving (1 Kings 6); the Ark of the Covenant with its mercy seat and cherubim; the pot of manna and Aaron's rod preserved in the place; the eternal fire on the altar. Now all of that is gone, victims of Babylonia's destructive armies, and dim old eyes can only fill with tears at the loss and at the dismal replacement of what they once knew. Oh yes, the people in Haggai's time could have empathized with our disappointments about the church.

But Haggai's contemporaries forgot, and we forget, that the glory of the temple and of the church is not the magnificent building or the wondrous ritual or the influence of the congregation in society. Rather the glory of the temple and of the church is the presence of the Lord in their midst. And that is the message that Haggai brings to his disheartened people and to us. "Take courage ... take courage ... take courage," God commands three times in our text. "Work, for I am with you," as I have always been since the time of your redemption. "My Spirit abides among you; fear not" (vv. 4-5). God is with Judah; he has not abandoned her, despite her sin and exile and desperate situation. And God is with us in his church, despite all that we have done to disrupt his purpose and to be undeserving of his presence. God is with us, his glory still in the midst of his church.

Do we realize, then, what powers are available because that is true? The God who ignited the sun and flung the stars across millions of galaxies; the Lord who created a people named Israel for himself and who has preserved their life through 3,000 years; the King who defeated all the powers of evil and death on Easter morn and who still reigns as Ruler of heaven and earth; the Shepherd who first gave you the breath of life and who has watched over you and guided you through all your sufferings and joys; that God is still in his church, still in our midst, still lending us his power through his mighty Spirit to rebuild and to prosper his church. Do we not, then, have all the resources we need in him to work without fear?

More, can we not have great expectations, rather than sorrow, over the future that lies out there ahead of us and the church? Our text from Haggai is directed not only to Judah's present condition, but also to her future. "In a little while," the Lord proclaims. In that indefinite time in God's future working, he will shake the heavens and the earth and all the cosmos, to fill a new temple with treasures and a new Jerusalem with abundant life (*shalom* in the Hebrew, v. 9), and his kingdom will be present on earth even as it is in heaven. Haggai's message reaches out to that eschatological time when God's good purpose for his world will be complete, and all nations will come to his worship.

We have the same expectation and same hope in the church, do we not? That there lies out ahead of us all, not the sometimes desperate situations that we now find in our world, not the meagerness of our faith and the faults of our sins, not the turmoil of nations and the rule of the evil and proud, but the rule of the one God who has triumphed over all principalities and powers in our crucified and risen Lord. The whole New Testament — and indeed, the Old, and Haggai here — announce it. That God is not through with us; that his purpose goes steadily forward; that finally every knee shall bow and every tongue confess that Jesus Christ is Lord, to God's glory. And our disappointments, our despair over the future, our tears, our sufferings will be things of the past. And earth will be fair, and life will be good and whole, and God will be our all in all.

So take courage, good people of faith, take courage. Work in his church and fear not. For the Lord God Almighty is in our midst, and his Spirit abides among us.

Proper 28

Isaiah 65:17-25

This text forms the last portion of the long judgment-salvation oracle that is contained in Isaiah 65. It comes from Israel's post-exilic period, when for the first time in the Old Testament, the Lord divides his covenant people into two groups, those who will be judged and those who will be saved. The difference between them is that one group has depended on the Lord for its life, while the other has not and has deliberately turned away from its Lord (cf. 65:1, 11-12). Trust, faith marks the way by which God's saving acts will be received.

Because of the way verse 17 is used in the New Testament, in Revelation 21:1 and 2 Peter 3:11-13, it has often been held that it characterizes the beginning of apocalypticism in the Old Testament, in which our present evil history is abandoned and God creates an entirely new heaven and earth. However, there is no abandonment of this world in our text. Verse 17 reads in the Hebrew, "For behold, I am creating ..." that is, God's act of re-creation has already begun, as God works gradually in human history, and the salvation that is promised is spelled out in the concrete circumstances of Jerusalem's everyday life.

In contrast to the New Testament, there is no mention of eternal life here. The Old Testament has no statement of resurrection or life after death until the time of the second century B.C. Book of Daniel (Daniel 12:2-3). There are earlier hints that even death cannot separate the faithful from God (Job 19:25-27; Psalm 73:23-26; Isaiah 25:6-8). But after all, the incarnation and resurrection have not yet taken place. Therefore our text deals concretely only with the saving work of God in this world.

The transformations that God here proclaims that he will work in the life of the faithful are marvelous in their promise. To the suffering faithful (cf. chs. 58 and 59), the Lord promises that he

237

will replace their distress and weeping with joy and gladness (65:19). And that gladness will come from many things. For example, no longer will there be premature death, either of infants or of elderly (v. 20). To the Hebrew mind, long life was a gift of God, who is the Source of all life (cf. Deuteronomy 4:40; Job 5:26). Death was seen as a natural part of life and was accepted rather peacefully (cf. Genesis 25:8), unless it was premature or violent. Then it was understood as a judgment or curse from God. The implication is, therefore, that all of the faithful will live in the favor of the Lord.

The Lord also promises that his people (note "my people" in v. 19) will never again suffer the loss of their houses and vineyards and property, either through the ravages of war, or, more importantly, because of the greed and injustice of the proud and powerful. Many of the prophets condemned the injustices perpetrated upon the poor by corrupt courts of law, that seized the property of the helpless in payment of debts, while throwing them into prison or selling them into slavery. Such injustices and violence will never again take place, the Lord promises.

Further, our text proclaims that those faithful to the Lord "shall not labor in vain" (v. 23). Rather, they will reap the rewards of their labor. One of the curses on Adam in the story of the Fall in Genesis 3 is that he will no longer experience reward from his work commensurate with the effort he puts into it. His sweat, his toil, his drudgery will be meaningless and without due reward.

Perhaps that promise of meaningful work furnishes the most relevant entrance into this text for the preacher, for there are a lot of people in our times who see no point in the way they earn their daily bread or in the way they have to struggle. As has been said, they lead lives of "quiet desperation," in which all that they do has no meaning or satisfactory recompense. They experience the same old routine, day after day, with no purpose to it all.

Indeed, even parents can feel that way when they spend hours of anxiety and toil raising their children, only to have them turn out badly. As one mother put it, "We raise our kids, and someone else tears them down." Nothing seems to bear good fruit. And of course, all the labor, all the anxiety, all the struggle to make something of life, ends in death, and we are gone, forgotten in just a few short years.

But the promise of God in our text is that there will be a permanence to human life — "like the days of a tree," says verse 22, which is often a symbol of permanence in the Old Testament (cf. Psalm 92:12-14; Job 14:7-9). Honest work will render meaningful and lasting results, and labor will not be spent in vain.

Above all, verse 24 emphasizes that God will be near his faithful folk. Even before they pray, he will hear them, and even before they finish speaking, he will answer them. In contrast to those mentioned at the beginning of chapter 65, to whom God called but who never answered, those who trust in the Lord will find themselves in an intimate communion with their God, who will be sufficient for all their needs.

The New Testament did not err in the way it used the words of this chapter from Third Isaiah. For finally, the fulfillment of all of these promises from the Lord will come only when Christ does return to set up the Kingdom of God on earth, with its total transformation of our lives. We do in fact still suffer the violence and heartbreak of premature death of beloved infants and elderly. Our earth still knows the greed and injustice of the powerful and proud, and the rape and pillage of war. We still do know the impermanence of life in an era of dizzying change. Many still suffer the meaninglessness of the work they are doing.

But God has promised to transform it all. He made that promise to Israel — a promise that is now extended to all his faithful covenant folk through his Son Jesus Christ. And ours is a God who always keeps his promises. In the New Testament message, there rings out the assurance of triumph over death, over suffering, over evil, over all, and yes, the reward for labor in the Lord. "Therefore, my beloved," writes Paul, "be steadfast, immovable, always abounding in the work of the Lord, knowing that in the Lord your labor is not in vain" (1 Corinthians 15:58). If we trust God in Jesus Christ, we can know that is true.

Christy the King

Jeremiah 23:1-6

Both Luke (15:3-7; 19:10) and John (10:11-12) characterize our Lord as the Good Shepherd. And Matthew, Mark, and Luke all use the title of King to describe him. Actually, the two terms, shepherd and king, are synonymous, because kings, throughout the scriptures, are known as the shepherds of their people.

Thus our text is dealing with the rulers of Israel, and it is made up of two separate oracles (vv. 1-4 and 5-6) that have been editorially included in Jeremiah's long section concerning the kings and leaders of Judah in the last decades of her life (Jeremiah 21:11—23:8).

The first oracle, verses 1-4, pronounces woe on the bad king and leaders of the people who have not cared for the flock of Judah. The reference is probably to the despot Jehoiakim (609-598 B.C.), whose evil deeds of forced labor and injustice and oppression are described in Jeremiah 22:13-17. That woe is pronounced on Jehoiakim indicates that he is as good as dead. But the oracle then continues with the promise that the exiles of Judah who were carried into Babylonia in 597 and 587 B.C. will be returned by God to their own country and have placed over them shepherds who will care for their welfare.

The second oracle of salvation, in verses 5-6, goes even further. In the future, the Lord will raise up a descendant of David to occupy the throne. He will be a righteous king, whose name will be "The Lord is our righteousness." He will rule wisely, with justice and righteousness, so that all in a reunited Israel and Judah will be secure and "saved." The latter word has as its root meaning "to be spacious," "to have room," and this promise is stating that a new Israel, returned to its land, will have room to live in full abundance and security. No longer will enemies threaten or destroy them. And no longer will they live under the judgment of God. Rather, they will live in favor with God, guided and sustained by his chosen ruler.

There are centuries of background that lie behind these passages. According to 2 Samuel 7, in the tenth century B.C., God promises David that there will never be lacking an heir to sit upon the davidic throne. And the life and fortunes of the people of Israel are from that time forth bound up with the character of the davidic king. He is the "corporate personality" of Israel. If he is a good king, therefore, ruling in righteousness and justice according to the commandments of God, the people will be counted righteous in God's eyes. But if the king is evil, then the people also will be counted as evil and will be judged by the Lord.

But what does it mean to be "righteous," according to the scriptures? "Righteousness" is always a relational term, and it consists in fulfilling the demands of a relationship. Every relationship — with parents or siblings, with colleagues or compatriots — brings with it different demands. The primary demands of our relationship with God, for example, are to love and trust him, so that we obey his commands.

But the primary duties of a righteous king in Israel are spelled out rather clearly in many passages, particularly in the Royal Psalms such as Psalm 72. The righteous king, says that Psalm, delivers the needy and poor, and has pity on the weak and saves those in need. He turns aside oppression and violence and values the life of his people (Psalm 72:12-14). In Ezekiel 34, in negative terms, the "shepherds" of Israel are condemned by God because "the weak you have not strengthened, the sick you have not healed, the crippled you have not bound up, the strayed you have not brought back, the lost you have not sought, and with force and harshness you have ruled them" (Ezekiel 34:4). Or in Isaiah 11, the righteous king does "not judge by what his eyes see, or decide by what his ears hear; but with righteousness he shall judge the poor, and decide with equity for the meek of the earth" (Isaiah 11:3-4).

The picture, wherever we look in the scriptures, is of a ruler who reigns in mercy and kindness, in justice and concern for even the least of his people. That is the king that Jeremiah promises that the Lord will raise up in the future to rule over his people Israel.

Because the king will reign in such fashion, he will be a righteous king. And therefore his people too will be counted righteous in the eyes of God.

Throughout the centuries, the covenant people looked for such a king to be sent by God to rule over them. Of every ruler after the time of David and Solomon, they asked of the new occupant of the davidic throne, "Are you the one who will come? Or should we look for another?"

In such expectation, Israel was looking for its Messiah. For The word "Messiah" is taken from the Hebrew word, *masiah*, which simply means "anointed." Davidic kings were anointed in Israel, and the expectation of a Messiah was for an anointed davidic ruler, who would reign in justice and righteousness, in mercy and love for his people.

Israel's hopes for a Messiah to save them were dashed, however, by the Babylonian exile, when their davidic king was taken prisoner to Babylon. And yet, the hope persisted, and some even thought that Zerubbabel, a descendant of David, would be the Messiah in the post-exilic time of Haggai and Zechariah. But the ages stretched on, and in the New Testament, we still find faithful Jews "looking for the redemption of Israel" (Luke 2:38; cf. 24:21). The question we are left with, therefore, is: Did God ever fulfill this promise that we find in our text from Jeremiah? Did he ever raise up a davidic king, who would save the life of his people?

The Gospels tell us that God kept his promise. When Jesus of Nazareth rode into Jerusalem on that donkey, on what we call Palm Sunday, he was hailed as the Son of David (Matthew 21:9), and the disciples cried out, "Blessed is the King who comes in the name of the Lord! Peace in heaven and glory in the highest!" (Luke 19:38; cf. Mark 11:9-10). And when our Lord was crucified, even Pontius Pilate had to acknowledge that Jesus was the King of the Jews (John 19:19-22), the long-expected Messiah from Israel, sent to save his people.

Certainly we find in our Lord all of those qualities that Israel said would characterize its Messiah — the mercy and love, the justice and righteousness that belong to God's promised king. And in his righteousness, do we not find also our righteousness in the eyes of God? Because Jesus Christ took all of our wrongs, our evil, our sins, and our terribly human mistakes upon himself, and let them be nailed to the cross and buried with him, and then was raised triumphant over them all, we now are forgiven and counted righteous in the eyes of our God. So we can join in the confession that we find at the end of our text in Jeremiah, can't we? "The Lord is our righteousness." He is indeed. And because that is true, you and I can be saved.

Thanksgiving Day

Deuteronomy 26:1-11

Thanksgiving is a response to what God has done. It is not centered primarily in how we feel, so that there can be times when we do not feel thankful. And it is not an expression of gratitude for what we have been able to accomplish, so that we remain the subject of the action. No. Thanksgiving, according to the scriptures, has as its motivation, center, and subject the actions of the Lord. And because that is true, we can always give thanks.

Thanksgiving is, moreover, in the scriptures a public witness to the actions of God. The Israelites of the Old Testament never felt that God had been properly thanked for his deeds unless they told others about what God had done and thus glorified God's name in the eyes of others. So it is that we find in the Psalms of Thanksgiving public testimonies to what God has performed, and the necessity of telling others about those acts.

> *Come and hear, all you who fear God, and I will tell*
> *what he has done for me.*
> Psalm 66:16; cf. Psalm 116:14, 18-19

The case is similar here with regard to our text for the morning. There is no doubt in this passage as to who is the subject of thanks. It is "the Lord your God" — a phrase repeated eight times, and the whole passage centers on God's deeds. In fulfillment of his promise to the patriarchs (v. 3), God has given the worshiper the land (v. 1) and all its produce (v. 11). He has chosen the place where thanks is to be rendered, namely in Jerusalem (v. 2). He has multiplied the descendants of Israel, and delivered them from bondage in Egypt, leading them through the terrors of the wilderness, and bringing them into the promised land, flowing with milk and honey (vv. 5-9). And so God is to be thanked and praised in joy (v. 11) for all his saving acts.

245

That thanks takes the form of the offering of the first fruits of produce from the land which the Lord God has given the worshiper. In recognition of the fact that the land belongs not to Israel, but to the Lord (Leviticus 25:23; Exodus 20:8-11), the law of Israel stipulates that all first fruits of the ground are to be offered to the Lord (Exodus 23:19; 34:26). And that offering, here in our text, takes the form of a public ceremony in the temple, in which the worshiper brings his gifts and makes the public confession of faith that is found in verses 5-9.

The confession that we find in these latter verses is probably one of the oldest confessions to be found in the Old Testament. It follows the narrative of Israel's history that we find in the Hexateuch, or first six books, of the Bible. And by the events that are mentioned, it shows us what Israel considered to be the absolutely decisive acts of God in her past history: the wanderings of the patriarch Jacob, who went down to Egypt; the multiplication of the population in Egypt; the attention of God to his enslaved people's cries for deliverance; the Lord's redemption of them out of slavery, "with a mighty hand and an outstretched arm, with great terror, with signs and wonders"; and his gift of the promised land to them in the time of Joshua.

Those are the principal acts of God that formed Israel's faith in the beginning and that sustained her through all of the following years. None of them were acts on Israel's behalf that she deserved. And, as Deuteronomy 7:6-8 states, all were done by God for two reasons. First, he heeded Israel's cries for redemption from slavery simply because he chose Israel to be his special people and he loved them. Second, he redeemed Israel and led her to the promised land in order to fulfill the promise that he first gave to Abraham. At the core here of Israel's faith is a confession that testifies that her God is a faithful God, keeping his promise, and a loving God, bestowing his grace on a people who have done nothing to deserve it.

Are we not also able to make such a confession, that God has chosen us to be his people simply out of love, apart from any deserving on our part, and then has redeemed us also from our slavery — not our slavery in Egypt, but our slavery to sin and death by the cross and resurrection of Jesus Christ? We Christians too

246

have a past full of the saving acts of God, to which we can make grateful response on this Thanksgiving Day. We confess all of those acts every time we recite the Apostles' Creed together: "his only Son our Lord, who was born of the Virgin Mary, suffered under Pontius Pilate, was crucified, dead and buried. He descended into hell. The third day he rose again from the dead. He ascended into heaven and sitteth on the right hand of God the Father. From thence he shall come to judge the quick and the dead." Oh, yes, we too have a confession of faith that tells publicly of all the deeds that God has done on our behalf.

Some of you also have a private confession that you can make, do you not — an account of the acts of love that God has worked in your own particular life? How he has granted you gifts and good running over, preserved your spirit through trouble and suffering, guided you away from temptation, or given you the certain hope, when you have lost a loved one, that death never marks a final goodbye. I think we all could at this moment make a public acknowledgement of the mercies that God has shown to us. I hope you tell other people about those deeds of the Lord your God, and thus bring glory to his name.

But above all else, we Christians have those basic facts about God's acts in the life, death, and resurrection of Jesus Christ that form the very center, motivation, and content of our faith. And that brings us to the most startling aspect of our text for the morning.

If you will listen carefully to this text, you will notice that the pronouns suddenly change, as the confession is recited. The worshiper starts off talking about the past. "A wandering Aramean was my father; and he went down into Egypt ... and there he became a nation...." But then suddenly, the account becomes personal; the pronouns change: "And the Egyptians treated *us* harshly, and ... *we* cried to the Lord ... and the Lord heard *our* voice...." Suddenly the past is no longer past for this Israelite worshiper. It has become his present. He is there in Egypt; the Lord has delivered him from slavery, and brought him into the promised land.

And that is the way the story of our salvation in the Bible also works for us. When we read the New Testament accounts of the Last Supper, for example, that is not a meal taking place in the

247

past. Suddenly we are there, eating and drinking with our Lord, receiving his new covenant in his blood, but also hearing that one of us will betray him. Or when we hear the story of the crucifixion, are we not also there at the foot of the cross, hearing Jesus' final prayer, "Father, forgive them ..."? And do we not find ourselves also forgiven by that sacrifice? The Negro spiritual has it right, "Were you there when they crucified my Lord?" Yes, indeed, we were there. And "sometimes it causes me to tremble."

God's merciful acts of salvation, recorded for us in the scriptures, are not just past events. They are also deeds done for us right now, "this day," as our text says (v. 3). We now are chosen by God to be his special people. Our cries to him for deliverance are now, this day, heard by him. And we now, undeserving though we may be, are delivered from our slavery to all of our sins, and from our final slavery to the power of death.

So give thanks to God on this Thanksgiving Day, good Christians. For he has delivered us "with a mighty hand and an outstretched arm." Praise his name, and glorify him forever!

Index of Biblical Texts
in Canonical Order